Contents

Introduction

Have you ever felt like no one really gets what you're going through? Like your thoughts and feelings are just too complicated or too personal to share? If so, you're not alone—and this book was written just for you.

Being 14, 15, or 16 means that you're right in the heart of your teen years—you're definitely not a preteen anymore but not an adult yet, either. You may be questioning a lot right now, trying to figure things out and feeling a lot of emotions at once.

But in the midst of the uncertainty you may be feeling at times, there's one thing I know for sure: God wants to spend time with you. He cares deeply about every part of your life—even the messy, confusing, or hard-to-share parts. My prayer is that this book would spark real, honest conversations between you and God, giving you hope, confidence, and—most of all—a deep understanding of his love for you.

In these pages, you'll find wisdom and encouragement from the Bible to help you through this unique season of life. As a teen, I remember the struggle of figuring out who I was while working through all the emotions, questions, and experiences I was facing. Unfortunately, back then, I didn't really know Jesus. Church felt like more of a ritual than a chance to build a relationship with God.

But once I truly understood the gospel—the truth that Jesus died and rose again to have a full, vibrant relationship with me—everything changed. I realized that spending time with him wasn't some boring obligation. It was a way to receive the love, strength, and wisdom I needed to get through every challenge. I only realized this when I was 19, so I feel honored to have a chance, through this book, to share God's truths with you that I wish I'd known sooner.

The truth is, no one else has lived your story, but Jesus knows every part of it and understands you completely. You're stepping into a new season of independence and making more decisions for yourself now—how you spend your time after school, what interests you pursue, and how to engage with friendships, romantic relationships, social media, and more. This can feel both exciting and overwhelming. You need a steady foundation to stand on, and God wants to be that for you.

As we walk through this year together, my goal is to meet you in your day-to-day struggles and questions, take them seriously, and then point you to our Savior and the real-life help he offers in every single situation.

As a teen, I wanted to be seen fully, for all of who I am. I hated feeling underestimated, overlooked, or unheard. So as I write these words, I want you to know that I hear you. I see you. While I don't know you personally, I *do* know that you are beautifully complex, uniquely designed by God, and your thoughts, emotions, and struggles are incredibly real. God takes every part of you seriously, and so do I.

How would you describe your relationship with Jesus? Maybe you go to church regularly and know all of the popular Bible stories and some of the not-so-popular ones, but you're not quite sure what it means to walk with Jesus in your daily life. Maybe you have a close connection with him that you want to keep growing. Or maybe you're new to your faith, curious about what Jesus teaches and how it applies to you.

No matter where you are in your walk with Jesus, this book is for you. Let's get started and see what God has in store!

How to Use This Book

This book is designed to provide practical encouragement for each week of the year as you grow in your relationship with God. Each devotion covers a topic that matters in your life, paired with a Bible verse to help you discover God's guidance. At the end of each devotion, you'll find a few questions to think about, journal about, or discuss with a friend. Then, you'll see a simple prayer that asks for God's help as you navigate this area of life. (Feel free to keep the conversation with God going afterward!)

My hope is that each devotion will help you build your faith, practice having real conversations with God, and live out what you're learning in your everyday life. We can't cover everything you'll experience in your teens in just one book, but I can tell you that you will gain a better understanding of how to rely on God's presence, comfort, and wisdom, no matter what comes your way.

UNDERSTANDING GOD'S WORD

I pray that this book will help you fall in love with learning about God through his Word. Each devotion starts with a passage of Scripture to guide you to God's truth, but here are a few more tips for learning how to engage with the Bible:

★ *After reading the verse of the day,* try looking up the whole chapter to get the bigger picture and learn even more. And if you prefer listening, try an audio Bible—I love the Streetlights app! Hearing Scripture can bring it to life in a new way.

- ★ *Feeling distracted?* Pause and pray. Ask God to give you focus, to help you feel his presence, and to show you something new in his Word.
- ★ *Focus on quality over quantity.* Remember, reading the Bible is about meeting with God, not completing a homework assignment. Read intentionally and thoughtfully—don't worry about how much or how little you've read.
- ★ *Make it fun:* Write out a passage that's speaking to you with colorful pens, stick a Bible verse in your locker, or challenge a friend to memorize a Bible verse with you.
- ★ *Want to know Jesus more?* The Gospels (Matthew, Mark, Luke, and John) will give you the clearest picture of his heart. Try reading one chapter a day or whenever you're able!

In Weeks 10 and 11, we'll discuss more Bible study and prayer tips to help you along the way.

STAYING MOTIVATED AND FOCUSED

Let's be honest: sticking to a routine to spend time with God isn't always easy. Even when we know how much we'll be blessed by our time with God, it can be hard to stay focused and motivated. Here are some ideas to help:

- ★ *Keep it visible:* Leave this book in a place where you'll see it often—by your bed, near your toothbrush, or wherever makes sense for you. A visual reminder can help you stay on track. You could even set your phone wallpaper to a favorite verse to keep God's Word on your mind.

- ★ *Plan ahead:* Choose a day and time when you'll read each week. Pick a time when you feel awake and clear-headed, and when other obligations won't get in the way. Maybe you know you always need a little extra inspiration on a Monday morning, or perhaps a weekend makes the most sense when you're feeling relaxed and rested.
- ★ *Stick to it:* Once you've chosen a day and time, add it to your calendar or set an alarm on your phone.
- ★ *Make it special:* Pair your devotional time with a routine in your life that you enjoy. Make it a part of your evening wind-down or your weekend breakfast. For me, cozying up with a hot drink and my Bible makes time with God something I truly look forward to.
- ★ *Get support:* Include a friend in your weekly devotion time, or ask a family member to check in with you and cheer you on.
- ★ *Remember the why:* Spending time with God isn't just another chore on your list. It's a chance to receive his peace, wisdom, and encouragement, and it can turn your whole day around!

Let each devotion be a reminder that God loves spending time with you and he's ready to fill your heart with everything you need to face the week ahead.

TEEN DEVOTIONAL for GIRLS

52 WEEKS OF INSPIRING DEVOTIONS, SCRIPTURE, AND PRAYERS FOR TEENAGERS

Ellie Hunja

Zeitgeist Young Adult · New York

For Keziah, may you feel surrounded by
God's love and mine, always.

In memory of Phillip and Terrance, whose
joy and faith in Jesus in their teen years
ignited my own. I'm forever grateful.

Zeitgeist Young Adult
An imprint of Zeitgeist™
A division of Penguin Random House LLC
1745 Broadway, New York, NY 10019
zeitgeistpublishing.com
penguinrandomhouse.com

Copyright © 2025 by Penguin Random House LLC

Penguin Random House values and supports copyright. Copyright fuels creativity, encourages diverse voices, promotes free speech, and creates a vibrant culture. Thank you for buying an authorized edition of this book and for complying with copyright laws by not reproducing, scanning, or distributing any part of it in any form without permission. You are supporting writers and allowing Penguin Random House to continue to publish books for every reader. Please note that no part of this book may be used or reproduced in any manner for the purpose of training artificial intelligence technologies or systems.

Zeitgeist™ is a trademark of Penguin Random House LLC.

Except where otherwise noted, Scripture quotations are taken from the Holy Bible, New International Version®, NIV®. Copyright © 1973, 1978, 1984, 2011 by Biblica Inc.™ Used by permission of Zondervan. All rights reserved worldwide (www.zondervan.com). The "NIV" and "New International Version" are trademarks registered in the United States Patent and Trademark Office by Biblica Inc.® Scripture quotations marked (NLT) are taken from the Holy Bible, New Living Translation, copyright © 1996, 2004, 2015 by Tyndale House Foundation. Used by permission of Tyndale House Publishers, Carol Stream, Illinois 60188. All rights reserved.

ISBN: 9798217151554
Ebook ISBN: 9798217151547

Printed in the United States of America

1st Printing

Illustrations © by MarushaBelle/Shutterstock.com
Book design by Aimee Fleck
Author photograph © by Michael Sanville
Edited by Kim Suarez

The authorized representative in the EU for product safety and compliance is Penguin Random House Ireland, Morrison Chambers, 32 Nassau Street, Dublin DO2 YH68, Ireland. https://eu-contact.penguin.ie

PART ONE

Faith Foundations

After he put
them all out, he
took the child's
father and
mother and the
disciples who
were with him,
and went in
where the child
was. He took
her by the hand
and said to her,
"Talitha koum!"
(which means
"Little girl, I say
to you, get up!").
Immediately
the girl stood
up and began
to walk around
(she was twelve
years old). At
this they were
completely
astonished.

MARK 5:40–42

Our entire lives transform when we are born again.

The 12-year-old girl from this week's Scripture experienced the ultimate miracle: she was dead, and Jesus raised her back to life! Imagine waking up to your family's shock and joy as you stand and begin to walk!

How would your life change after that? Would you feel like you're alive for a reason? What would it mean to realize that Jesus cared so much about you that he came to bring you back to life?

Here's the amazing truth: Jesus still raises the dead today. When we put our faith in him, we are reborn! He brings us to life in him—a miracle just as extraordinary as the one we read about today.

When I put my faith in Jesus, my whole life was transformed. Sure, it didn't look as dramatic as a physical resurrection, but I can look back and see it was just as real! After years of longing for unconditional love and acceptance, the love of Jesus helped me heal from past rejections and feel safe and secure. His love changed my heart and made me want to live for his purpose instead of what I thought was best for my life.

Our salvation can be easy to take for granted if we don't stop and think about the ways God has transformed us. Today, take a moment to really reflect on the miracle God performed when he gave you brand-new life in him.

And if you've never placed your faith in him, maybe today is the day. If you're ready to experience new life in Jesus, to leave the old you behind, and to walk in his unconditional love and perfect peace, all you have to do is believe. There's no perfect script to follow. In your own words, thank Jesus for dying for your sins and tell him you're ready to live for him. He is ready to embrace you with open arms and great joy!

1. How do you think the miracle in this week's Scripture impacted this community and how they saw Jesus?
2. What does it mean to you to be spiritually dead because of your sins but then brought to life by faith in Jesus? When was the first time you realized this and believed it? Or, if you haven't yet, what's holding you back?
3. How does knowing you have "new life" in Jesus change the way you see yourself and your purpose in life?
4. What are some things you may need to leave behind in your "old life" in order to really live for Jesus?

PRAYER God, thank you for saving me and giving me new life in you. Please help me to be amazed at this gift of grace, allowing your mercy and love to transform me. Help me to never forget the sacrifice you made and to find purpose and direction in you daily.

> *For God so loved the world that he gave his one and only Son, that whoever believes in him shall not perish but have eternal life. For God did not send his Son into the world to condemn the world, but to save the world through him.*
>
> **JOHN 3:16–17**

Because of Jesus' sacrifice, nothing can take away God's love from me.

I was sitting at my lab table in biology class one day, "whispering" some gossip to my lab partner about a classmate with whom I had a love-hate relationship. Unfortunately, I'm terrible at whispering, so my "frenemy" (who sat right behind us—oops!) heard every word.

I was mortified—the kind of shame that twists your stomach into knots and makes your face feel hot. I desperately wished I could shrink or disappear. Not only did I upset my classmate, but my friends judged me for being so careless and rude.

But this week's verse reminds us that even when we feel shame and condemnation because of our mistakes, Jesus didn't come to condemn us; he came to save us. So once you believe in him, shame, guilt, and condemnation no longer have power over you. When you feel the weight of shame sitting on your chest or hear an inner voice saying you're a bad person or you'll never measure up, you can know for sure it's not from God. Our loving Father is patient and kind, and will always remind you of the truth of his forgiveness.

No matter how many mistakes we make, God isn't shaking his head in disapproval—he's opening his arms to forgive us and help us through it. We are forgiven because of God's deep, sacrificial love for us, and because we are "washed clean" by the blood of Jesus, we can run into his loving arms without shame. Jesus' sacrifice ensures that once we confess our sins to him, nothing stands between us and God.

We're all works in progress, but that doesn't change God's pure delight in us. He celebrates every step you take toward him and loves you fully, even as you grow. So if your sin, past or present, leaves you wondering how God feels about you, you can rest assured: he loves you completely and unconditionally.

1. How does the truth of this week's verse challenge any feelings of shame or guilt that you might be dealing with?
2. Think about a time when you felt God's forgiveness. How did that moment impact your relationship with him?
3. How can remembering God's delight in you—even as you grow—encourage you to keep pursuing him?
4. Is there someone in your life dealing with feelings of shame? How could you encourage them with this week's scripture?

PRAYER God, sometimes your love for me feels too good to be true. It's hard to comprehend that no matter what mistakes I make, you will always keep loving me. Help me to embrace the truth that Jesus' sacrifice on the cross took away every barrier that stood between you and me. When I sin, help me to run to you, remember what you did on the cross, and receive your loving embrace.

"Child of God" is my most important identity on this earth.

The first time I read this Scripture, I couldn't get over the exclamation points. They're rare in the Bible, so they make this truth leap off the page. It's as if God is saying, "Don't miss this! Let it amaze you!" The Creator of the universe loves you so much that he calls you his child!

Child of God. More than any other label or identity, this is what defines you and me and everyone who places their faith in Jesus. If you take just one truth from this book after our year together, I hope it's this—that you are a beloved child of God, wholly accepted, forgiven, and adored by a Heavenly Father who will never leave you, never give up on you, and never stop pursuing you.

When I was a teen, my life was full of changes and big decisions that shook my core. I asked myself questions like, *Who am I? What's my purpose? How do I fit in this world?*

But when I got to know God and leaned into my identity as his child, I found a sense of stability that nothing else could offer. In the coming weeks, we'll discover biblical truths to ground you in your faith and explore what God says about the big questions

See what great love the Father has lavished on us, that we should be called children of God! And that is what we are! The reason the world does not know us is that it did not know him.

1 JOHN 3:1

16

you're grappling with. Thankfully, God not only has all the answers, but he walks with you and lives within you as you navigate every high and low. His constant presence, love, and wisdom are with us every step of the way.

This year, I pray that you'll grow in trusting him and finding unshakable security in who you are: his beloved daughter.

1. What does it mean to you to be called a "child of God"? How does this identity affect the way you see yourself?

2. Take a moment to reflect on the phrase, "See what great love the Father has lavished on us." How have you experienced God's love recently?

3. Do you believe that God's love for you is unconditional and unchanging? If not, what doubts or fears hold you back from fully embracing that truth?

4. If you truly embraced being a beloved child of God, how would your life look different? What small step can you take this week to live in that truth?

PRAYER God, I want to truly know the depths of your love for me. Help me to understand how fully you embrace me as your child, so that I can face every challenge knowing that you will never, ever leave my side. Show me how you want to help me grow to trust you more this year.

Yet to all who did receive him, to those who believed in his name, he gave the right to become children of God—children born not of natural descent, nor of human decision or a husband's will, but born of God.

JOHN 1:12–13

God is a good Father, and he wants to show me the depth of his love.

The moment you believed in God, he adopted you as his child. Unlike earthly parents, who all have their flaws, God is perfect. His love is unconditional, and he has endless compassion, patience, presence, and everything else we need.

But let's be honest: it can be hard to picture a truly perfect Father when we live in a world full of imperfect relationships. And if your earthly father or parental figure has let you down or isn't a part of your life, it might be even harder to embrace God as a loving, dependable father.

Take a moment to think of the best qualities of the people who've cared for you. Maybe they're great listeners, or they always show up, or they know how to make you feel special. Now, picture these qualities multiplied to infinity! That's how much God wants to love, provide for, and comfort you.

And no matter what disappointments you've experienced with your earthly parents, you can rest assured that God can heal them. If you've felt criticized, God offers grace. If you've felt rejected, he welcomes you with open arms. If you've faced instability, he is steady, unchanging, and always dependable. If you've felt you had to earn love, know that God loved you before you ever existed. There's nothing you can do to make him love you more—or less!

God wants you to know him as a good Father. If that feels difficult, tell him that and ask him to reveal his love to you in personal ways. The Bible is clear that you are so deeply wanted and chosen by God. Invite him to show you the depth of his perfect love.

1. How do you currently view God as your Father? Does he feel close, or distant?
2. How has your relationship with your earthly parents or care-givers shaped the way you think about God?
3. What qualities would you wish for in a perfect parent? How does it feel to know that God embodies all those qualities and more?
4. Think of a time when someone you looked up to let you down. How can God's love and perfect character help to heal that area of your life?
5. What does it mean to you that you are wanted and chosen by God? Does this change the way you see yourself?

PRAYER God, it's hard to truly understand your perfect love when the world is less than perfect. But I don't want to limit how I see you just because people have let me down. Today, I pray that you would show me how deep your love is for me. Help me to feel your warm embrace and to see your patience, your grace, and how dependable you truly are.

If you declare with your mouth, "Jesus is Lord," and believe in your heart that God raised him from the dead, you will be saved.

ROMANS 10:9

WEEK 5

I can trust God to be a good and loving Lord and Savior.

When we put our faith in Jesus, he becomes our Lord and Savior—a phrase you've probably heard before. You might even have said it yourself. But what does it actually mean, and how does it change how we live? Let's take a look.

"Lord" means master or ruler. Putting our faith in Jesus means accepting that we are not the bosses of our lives—Jesus is. We do what he says because we trust our Creator's wisdom above our own.

A "Savior" is someone who rescues others from danger. When we say we're "saved," it means we believe that Jesus saved us from sin, death, and eternal separation from God. Jesus lived a perfect, sinless life, died on the cross in our place, and then rose from the dead to defeat the power of death once and for all. This, the greatest news of all, is called the gospel.

If you declare that Jesus is Lord and believe that he died and rose again to give you a new life, you are saved! Praise God! There's nothing more you need to do—no hoops to jump through, no rituals to perform. You're a believer, forever connected to God, and you'll live with him eternally in heaven.

Letting Jesus truly be our Lord and Savior isn't always easy, though. Trusting him as Lord over my decisions was (and still is) a struggle! It's tempting to want to make our own rules, especially when we see everyone around us doing their own thing.

I used to wonder, "Is it *really* that bad to drink?" or "Is it *that* big of a deal to lie?" I trusted my own ability to weigh the pros and cons more than I trusted God's reasons for his commands. But living as a Christian means letting God take the lead, trusting in Jesus' sacrifice instead of our own efforts, and truly believing that he is a good and loving Father whose commands are for our good.

Let this truth sink in: Jesus' love and sacrifice have given you everything you need. Let him lead your life, knowing he is both your Lord and Savior—the One who loves you deeply, saves you completely, and guides you faithfully every step of the way.

1. Have you declared that Jesus is your Lord and Savior? If not, is there something holding you back?
2. How does viewing Jesus as your Savior change the way you see your relationship with God?
3. When is it hardest for you to let Jesus lead your life?
4. What is one way you can practice trusting God's wisdom instead of your own this week?

PRAYER God, please help me to see you as the Lord of my life and the Savior of my soul. When I'm struggling to let you take the lead, show me how trustworthy you are. Remind me of the depths of your unconditional love that you showed on the cross. Thank you for saving me and leading me.

Jesus is my real and present help, no matter what I'm going through.

God is our refuge and strength, an ever-present help in trouble.

PSALM 46:1

Where do you run to when life gets tough? Maybe you call a family member or your best friend for advice. Maybe you turn on your favorite show and binge your favorite snacks, hoping you'll feel better. Or maybe you pray.

A lot of people think prayer is pointless—that we're just talking to ourselves. Some might say that it's ridiculous to believe that God is real, that he hears us, and that he answers.

But the truth is, everyone believes in something. We're all searching for hope and trying to make sense of life. For some, that's faith in God. For others, it's faith in astrology, tarot cards, crystals, manifestation, or whatever else they trust to guide and empower them. Every single human heart is searching for something to place their faith in.

When I was in high school, I looked everywhere for guidance. I read about different religions and spiritual ideas, mixing and matching until I thought I'd found what worked for me. But when I truly embraced the gospel for the first time at 19 years old, I realized that Christianity offers something that nothing else can: a real relationship with a *living* God.

God isn't distant or abstract. He became human so he could fully understand what it's like to live our lives. Only Jesus knows us completely—our joys, struggles, fears, and dreams. Everything else in this world was created, but God is the Creator. He existed before time began, and, in his perfect love, he stepped into our world as Jesus to show how far he'd go to save us.

You don't have to run anywhere else for comfort or guidance. God is present, living, and active, and only he can bring you the peace your heart longs for, right when you need it most.

1. Where do you usually turn when life gets tough? Why?
2. Have you ever experienced God's presence during a difficult time? How did it impact you?
3. Why do you think so many people look to things like astrology, tarot, crystals, or manifestation for guidance and power? How is a relationship with God different from all of these?
4. Do you ever struggle to believe that prayer works? What might help you grow your trust in God in this area?
5. What's one area of your life where you need to trust God more? Take time to pray about it today.

PRAYER God, sometimes I don't know where to run for help. I'm not always sure that you're listening, or that you can really help my situation. Please show me that you are living and active, always ready to hear me and show up for me. Help me to trust that you care for me and that you're the only one who can truly help me when nothing else can.

WEEK 7

My worth is rooted in God's sacrificial love for me.

I've questioned my worth countless times—when I don't measure up to society's impossible standards, when I fall short of my goals, and especially when I experience the sting of rejection. As a teen, my first heartbreak left me asking myself, *Why am I not enough? What else is my ex looking for that I don't have?*

Maybe you've been there too—left out, overlooked, or convinced that you'll never measure up. But this week's verse reminds us that Jesus came for *you*. He came for the brokenhearted, the rejected, and the weary. He brings freedom to captives and joy to those drowning in despair. Whatever has stolen your joy—failure, rejection, or shame—has no power over the One who turns ashes into beauty.

Society may question your value or worth, but God will *never* reject you. As his daughter, he calls you worthy, and his word is final.

You might think, "Worthy? But I'm a sinner! God is the one who's worthy." And that's true, but it's only half of the story. Here's the rest: long before time began, God had already decided that you were *worth* rescuing. He chose to sacrifice his only Son to

The Spirit of the Sovereign LORD is on me, because the LORD has anointed me to proclaim good news to the poor. He has sent me to bind up the brokenhearted, to proclaim freedom for the captives and release from darkness for the prisoners [. . .] and provide for those who grieve in Zion— to bestow on them a crown of beauty instead of ashes, the oil of joy instead of mourning, and a garment of praise instead of a spirit of despair.

ISAIAH 61:1,3

save you—not because you earned it, but because of his perfect love and mercy.

God didn't just call you "worthy" with words—he proved it with his actions on the cross. Your worth is rooted in who he is and who you are to him. And because he's the Creator of the universe—and of you—he gets the final say.

So when rejection whispers lies, remember this truth: God has called you worthy, and what he says about you will never change.

1. What situations or relationships make you question your worth?

2. When you feel rejected, what lies do you tend to believe about yourself?

3. How does Jesus' sacrifice on the cross demonstrate your worth in God's eyes? Have you fully accepted that truth in your heart?

4. Who are the people in your life who uplift and affirm your worth? How can you lean on them when you're struggling to believe the truth?

5. Who in your life needs to hear the message of their God-given worth? How can you share this truth with them this week?

PRAYER God, when I feel like I don't measure up, thank you for reminding me that your sacrifice shows I'm worth saving. You will never reject me. When I question my value, please remind me that you rescued me and declared my true worth, once and for all.

WEEK 8

> *You will seek me and find me when you seek me with all your heart.*
>
> **JEREMIAH 29:13**

Faith in Jesus isn't a spiritual to-do list; it's about having a heart that desires him.

When I first became a Christian and decided to get baptized, I set a huge goal: read the entire Bible before my baptism. But as the day got closer, I still had a massive chunk of the New Testament left to read, so I panicked. I started skimming, racing through verses without really absorbing them.

When I reached the last chapter, I felt victorious—"I did it!" But deep down, I knew I had missed something. I thought meeting my goal made me a "good" Christian, but I was way more focused on checking a box than actually connecting with God.

Reading the Bible is a great goal, but the *why* behind it matters even more. God doesn't want us to read his Word just because we're "supposed to"; he wants us to grow closer to him. We read God's Word to know his love and be transformed from the inside out.

This week's verse reminds us that we find God when we seek him with all our hearts—not just our minds. Faith isn't about perfect routines or completing spiritual checklists. It's about a heart that genuinely desires to know God.

That could look different each day. Maybe one day, you pour your heart out in prayer but don't open your Bible. Another day, you have a powerful worship experience at church that inspires you to read chapters and chapters of his Word when you get home. Other days, you may wrestle with a difficult verse and find clarity through a sermon or Bible study.

Faith in Jesus doesn't look one particular way—it's about the heart behind your actions. When you wholeheartedly desire to know God more, he promises you'll find him.

1. How does your faith shape the way you live right now?
2. Do you ever feel like you're going through the motions with God? How can you begin to pursue him in a heartfelt way?
3. Think of a time you felt especially close to God. What do you think made that time special?
4. How do you typically spend time with God? Do you think it's helping you connect with him in a genuine way?
5. Is there someone in your life who can encourage you as you grow closer to God? Consider asking them how they increase their desire for God when it's not coming naturally.

PRAYER God, I want deeper intimacy with you. I don't want our relationship to be distant or just based on checking off a to-do list. I want to spend time with you, to enjoy your presence, and to get to know you in your Word. Would you meet me today? When I'm feeling distracted or when my desire for you feels dried up, please renew my excitement for you and show me all the beauty that our relationship has in store.

Thomas said to him, "Lord, we don't know where you are going, so how can we know the way?" Jesus answered, "I am the way and the truth and the life. No one comes to the Father except through me."

JOHN 14:5–6

Jesus deserves to be at the center of our lives, not an afterthought.

After three years of walking with Jesus, the disciples were distraught. Their beloved teacher was about to be crucified, and they couldn't imagine life without him!

I wish I always felt as passionate as the disciples. If I'm being honest, some days I treat Jesus like more of an afterthought. But his words in this week's passage give us three reasons why he deserves to be at the center of our lives.

Jesus is **the way**. Jesus is the only path to God—apart from him, there's no way to have a right relationship with the Father. And because he lived a perfect, sinless life, he is the ultimate example of how to live for God's glory.

Jesus is **the truth**. Jesus is the Word of God made flesh (John 1:14). Everything Jesus taught, lived, and died for reveals God's heart to us and helps us separate the lies of the world and the enemy from God's truth.

Jesus is **the life**. Jesus is the source of all life, both physical and spiritual. When we trust him, we receive eternal life, which allows us to know our Creator personally and face every challenge with his strength.

If we really believe Jesus is the Way, the Truth, and the Life, we can't only spend time with him at church or whenever we get around to it. We can't treat him like a backup plan, making our own decisions until things go wrong and we need him. And we can't treat the Bible like a buffet, choosing the verses we like but ignoring the ones that challenge us to grow.

If you struggle with any of these habits (I know I do!), ask Jesus to show you that he *is* your life. Trust that when you put him at the center, you will see his goodness and grace flow into every area of your life.

1. When you think about your relationship with Jesus, do you see him as the center or as an add-on? Why?
2. In what areas of your life are you relying on your own strength instead of trusting Jesus completely?
3. How often do you turn to Jesus for wisdom and guidance in your day-to-day decisions? What could change if you begin to seek his direction more?
4. Think of a time when you treated Jesus as a "back-up plan." What would it have looked like to trust him fully from the start?
5. What's one habit you can start this week to center your life more on Jesus?

PRAYER Jesus, I'm thankful that you left us with such a powerful revelation of who you are. I confess that I don't always treat you as "the way"—sometimes I rely on my wisdom instead of your direction. Help me to truly put you at the center of everything I do.

How sweet are your words to my taste, sweeter than honey to my mouth! I gain understanding from your precepts, therefore I hate every wrong path. Your word is a lamp for my feet, a light on my path.

PSALM 119: 103–105

Reading God's Word helps me become more like him.

The world has no shortage of influencers who are trying to convince us to be like them. If we just use their product or follow their regimen, we'll be as pretty, popular, or successful as they are. I can't count the number of times I've clicked on those posts, hoping that their solution will somehow be different than all the ones that have let me down before.

Thankfully, there is only one person we need to model our lives after, and that is Jesus. We don't have to log onto social media to follow him. We have access to him and his direction for our lives through his Word, the Bible.

And the Bible isn't just a regimen to follow or a list of rules and regulations, do's and don'ts. God's Word is *life.*

The Bible isn't just words on a page; it's the living Word, God's voice speaking directly into our lives. As we read it, we learn who God is—faithful, loving, merciful, and so much more—and we grow to trust him more.

Through his Word, he guides us. When we're confused or conflicted, God's Word brings clarity and guidance, "a light to my path."

Most of all, though, God's Word transforms us. The Holy Spirit uses it to shape our hearts, helping us to desire what God desires and become more like Jesus.

When we open the Bible, we gain access to God's power to grow our faith, guide our decisions, and deepen our relationship with him. As you read, ask God to speak to your heart and trust that every word has the power to draw you closer to him.

Instead of reflection questions today, let's dive into the Bible to learn some basic study tips.

1. Set aside some time to study Psalm 119. This passage gives beautiful motivation for reading God's Word! It's long, so choose one section at a time.

2. Pray before you start, asking God to help you understand his Word and apply it to your life.

3. Start small. Like we discussed in the introduction, the quality of your Bible study time is always more important than the quantity of how many verses you cover.

4. After you read a passage, ask yourself the following questions. Consider writing the answers in a journal or notes app:

   - *What does this passage say?*
   - *What does it mean?*
   - *How can I apply it to my life?*

5. Ask questions. Jot down anything that doesn't make sense, and ask a trusted adult or friend to talk through it with you.

6. Be patient. Growing in our ability to study the Word takes time and practice. The goal is to connect with God. As long as you're doing that, you're succeeding!

PRAYER God, thank you for giving us your Word. Help me to truly see it as your voice speaking into my confusion and questions, like a lamp lights a path. Help me now as I practice studying your Word and applying it to my life. Help me believe in your power to transform me every time I open the Bible.

Prayer helps me align my heart with God's.

When I first became a Christian, I didn't know how I should pray. I thought some people were "better" at it because of their fancy words or tone of voice.

But this week's passage shows us that those things don't matter. In fact, earlier in Matthew 6, Jesus warns against praying in a certain way to try to impress others. Instead, he gives us a model for prayer—not to sound better but to align our hearts with God's heart.

So, how should we pray?

* **Begin with worship.** Praise God for who he is, not only because he deserves it but also because it encourages our hearts to remember how great God is and what a privilege it is to have a relationship with him! Playing worship music, lifting up your hands, or kneeling/bowing down can help you enter into worship.
* **Recognize that God knows best.** Praying for God's will to be done helps our hearts to desire his plans over our own.
* **Be honest about your needs.** Share your desires, feelings, and struggles with God. He cares about your everyday life.
* **Confess and forgive.** We ask for God's forgiveness so that nothing hinders our intimacy with

"This, then, is how you should pray:
"'Our Father in heaven, hallowed be your name, your kingdom come, your will be done, on earth as it is in heaven. Give us today our daily bread. And forgive us our debts, as we also have forgiven our debtors. And lead us not into temptation, but deliver us from the evil one.'"

MATTHEW 6:9–13

33

him and to remember that we're called to forgive others in the same way that he forgives us.

* **Ask for help to fight temptation.** Praying for strength to overcome temptation, our flesh, and the enemy keeps us dependent on our all-powerful God and not on our own limited strength.

While many of us have memorized the Lord's Prayer, remember that prayer isn't about the right words. God wants to hear from your heart. You can pray at any time and God doesn't care what words you use—he just wants to hear from you, his precious child.

1. Have you ever wondered how to pray or felt insecure about the way you pray? How did this week's devotion encourage you?
2. When you pray, do you spend time praising God? If not, how do you think that could improve your relationship with him?
3. Do you believe that God knows and cares about all of your needs? How could that truth impact the way you pray?
4. Is there something in your life right now that you need to be honest with God about? What's keeping you from sharing it with him?
5. How does it make you feel to know that, more than anything, God wants to hear your heart?

PRAYER God, I want to grow closer to you, but sometimes I don't know where to start. Please help me grow in my desire to pray. Help me to trust that you hear me and that you answer prayers. Help me to just pour out my heart to you, whatever that sounds like.

When I use my gifts and passions for God's purpose, I experience peace.

Have you ever looked at someone else and wished you could have their skills or abilities? I love to sing on my church's worship team, but I consider my voice to be "average." When I hear the voices of more talented singers, I often feel insecure. But one day, a friend mentioned that my energy and honesty during worship really encouraged her, and it got me thinking: What if I spent less time comparing myself to others and more time celebrating my own gifts?

I've noticed that when I'm feeling secure in my unique identity and gifts, I don't waste time on comparison. Instead, I'm excited to grow the gifts God has given me and find ways to glorify him in the process.

What unique gifts has God given you? The more you embrace who God made you to be, the stronger your sense of purpose and confidence will become. None of us is good at everything, but your unique gifts were placed in you for a reason—to impact the world for his glory.

Here's the truth: God has created you uniquely, with a purpose and strengths that are intentionally yours. No one else is like you—and that's exactly how God intended it.

For we are God's handiwork, created in Christ Jesus to do good works, which God prepared in advance for us to do.

EPHESIANS 2:10

And here's the most reassuring truth: everything good we achieve is part of God's plan. He's already prepared the path for us, as this week's verse reminds us, and we get to live it out by following his lead and asking him for direction. This process gives us deep satisfaction and joy.

When your passions align with God's purpose, something amazing happens—you experience a peace that guards your heart from comparison. In that peace, you find the confidence to play your part in his plan joyfully, knowing you're exactly who he created you to be.

What has God gifted you with? How can you use those gifts to honor him? This week's reflection questions will get you started in finding these answers.

1. What are you good at, and how do you feel when you use those gifts?
2. What unique challenges or experiences have you had, and how could God use them to impact others?
3. Are there any areas of your life where you wish you were more like someone else? How can you shift that thinking? (Here's an idea: write a daily affirmation that reminds you that you are exactly who God created you to be.)
4. How can you use your talents or unique characteristics to serve God and give him glory?

PRAYER God, there are days when I'm focused on the gifts I wish I had instead of the ones you gave me. Help me to grow a sense of contentment and even excitement in the unique way you created me. Give me insight into the special qualities you've placed inside of me and how I can use them to bring you glory.

PART TWO

My Inner World

The Holy Spirit empowers me to fight temptation.

> "So I say, walk by the Spirit, and you will not gratify the desires of the flesh. For the flesh desires what is contrary to the Spirit, and the Spirit what is contrary to the flesh. They are in conflict with each other, so that you are not to do whatever you want."
>
> **GALATIANS 5:16–17**

I remember shopping with some friends after school one day and one of them offered to steal makeup for us. Everyone else seemed okay with it, so I pointed out some eyeshadow I wanted, but I felt a tug-of-war in the pit of my stomach.

That battle between wrong and right is what the Bible calls the flesh (our sinful human nature) versus the Spirit, and it started the moment you believed in Jesus. Before that, we were spiritually "dead," so our human nature was in charge. Any good we did came from our own limited willpower.

But when we put our faith in Jesus' death and resurrection, God brought us "back to life" spiritually! The Bible calls this being "born again." (If you want to dig deeper, check out Romans 8!) Once we believe in Jesus, his Holy Spirit comes to live inside of us and empowers us to live differently.

Our human nature is self-centered. But as part of God's family, we've been given tools to overcome it. The Holy Spirit

★ places new desires in our heart, so we want to honor God more than we want to please ourselves

★ shows us the *why*—how sin may feel good in the moment but never benefits us in the long run

★ gives us strength that we would otherwise lack to make a choice that could be difficult or scary

The battle of wrong versus right is a spiritual one. And that's good news, because with the Holy Spirit, you have the power to win *every* time. Pausing and asking for God's help (like I should have done that afternoon with my friends) can give you the strength to make a choice that honors God.

You will stumble—that's part of being human. But each time you choose to follow the Spirit over your own desires, your self-control (a fruit of the Spirit!) grows, and you'll learn to rely on God's strength to walk in his ways.

1. Can you think of a time when you felt torn between doing what was right and giving in to temptation? What happened?

2. How do you feel when you lose a battle with your human nature? How can you turn to God in those moments instead of staying discouraged?

3. How does the truth of being born into God's family through Jesus affect the way you approach your daily struggles with sin?

4. Is there an area of your life where you've been relying on your own willpower instead of the Holy Spirit's strength? How can you ask God for help in that battle?

PRAYER God, sometimes I feel hopeless in the fight against my own desires. I want to live in a way that honors you, but temptation makes it difficult. Thank you for your Holy Spirit, who places new desires in my heart and gives me the power to resist temptation. God, help me to access your strength to walk in your Spirit.

When I know who I am in Christ, I can stay true to him when pressure comes.

Peer pressure can feel excruciating. We all want to belong and feel accepted, but sometimes that desire makes it hard to stay true to the values God calls us to live by.

A friend of mine still regrets a moment when he gave in to peer pressure. He lived down the street from a classmate who was always picked on at school. One evening, that classmate's family came over for dinner, and to my friend's surprise, they actually had a great time together! But the next day at school, instead of admitting it, he lied—pretending the visit was horrible just to fit in with his classmates. Looking back, he can't believe how easily he chose fitting in over showing God's love.

The truth is, standing firm in God's values isn't just about willpower—it's about transformation. This week's verse promises that when we walk with God, he renews our minds, helping us see the world through his eyes and to value what God values.

That transformation starts with knowing who you are in Christ. When you understand that you are fully known, fully loved, and created with

Do not conform to the pattern of this world, but be transformed by the renewing of your mind. Then you will be able to test and approve what God's will is—his good, pleasing, and perfect will.

ROMANS 12:2

43

purpose, that sense of identity gives you the confidence and strength to live for God, no matter what others think.

The next time you feel pressured to compromise, pause and ask yourself, "Does this align with God's values? Will this bring me closer to him and who he wants me to be, or further away?"

Over time, these questions will become second nature as God renews your mind and shapes your heart. The more you read and embrace his truth, the easier it becomes to live with integrity, resisting choices that conflict with who God created you to be.

You weren't meant to blend in—you were created to stand out as a light for Christ. Here are some questions that can help you discover how to live out your identity in him.

1. Can you think of a time when you chose pleasing others over staying true to God's values? How did you feel afterward?

2. Who in your life also loves God and wants to honor his values? How can they help you stay true to God's values when it's hard?

3. When do you feel most tempted to compromise your values? How can you prepare to stand strong in those moments?

4. How do the people closest to you see you? Ask them to name a few of your strengths or positive qualities. How might God want to use and grow these qualities to bless those around you?

PRAYER Lord, please help me to access your power to do what you want me to do and not just go along with what everyone else is doing. Help me to want to live for you more than I value the opinions of others and to keep my focus on growing closer to you.

True confidence comes from believing what God says about me.

We all have a human, sinful nature that makes assumptions based on what we see on the outside. But God calls us to look deeper to see what matters most: the heart.

When we place too much emphasis on external things like clothes, makeup, or physical features, a few things can happen. Some girls may feel judged because their outward appearance doesn't match others' standards or because they simply aren't into makeup or trends. Other girls might become so focused on fashion and beauty that they start to believe their value is only skin deep.

A friend shared with me that in high school, all her close friends were "petite, cute, and stylish," and she felt "tall, awkward, and less beautiful" in comparison. She'd often hunch over so she wouldn't stand out. My heart breaks to think of my beautiful friend shrinking herself to be more like someone else!

Here's the truth: your worth comes from being God's child, not from anyone's opinion of how you look. And guess what? God has *never* looked at you and wished you were someone else. God created you intentionally, and he delights in every part of your unique self.

The LORD does not look at the things people look at. People look at the outward appearance, but the LORD looks at the heart.

1 SAMUEL 16:7B

Fashion and makeup can be fun, creative outlets for self-expression, but they don't define us. When we rely on outward appearances to define our worth—or to judge others—we're building on a shaky foundation. True confidence comes from believing what God says about us—that we are loved and valued for who we are on the inside.

Remember, God sees your heart—and that's where true beauty lives.

1. Have you ever felt insecure about your appearance? Are you making choices based on what others will think or out of joyful self-expression?
2. Who or what influences your view of beauty? What would help you focus more on God's perspective?
3. Are there any toxic messages you've been receiving about beauty and appearances? What steps might you need to take to protect your heart from those messages?
4. What are some of your inner qualities that reflect God's character? How can you focus on those and let them shine?
5. Who in your life shines as an example of inner beauty? How can you celebrate and encourage them this week?

PRAYER God, thank you that you aren't superficial like the world can be. When I'm tempted to think that the right clothes or makeup will make me feel more valued, help me to remember that my true worth and value is in you. Help me to value inner beauty in myself and others and to rest in the truth that, whether I (or they) wear makeup or not, or wear the latest trends or not, we are all complete in Christ, and our foundation is built on your love.

WEEK 16

I can trust God to carry the worries that weigh me down.

High school can feel like a whirlwind. You're managing more academic pressure than ever before, along with extracurriculars, hobbies, friendships, and family. Maybe you're also working, volunteering, or helping out at home. For me, the weight felt crushing at times. My brain felt like it could never rest, frantic with thoughts about school, family issues, and my future plans.

So right now, I want you to pause. Take a deep breath and think about everything on your plate. It's a lot, and if no one else has told you lately, I see you. You're doing your best under a heavy load that others may try to minimize. God sees you, and he doesn't want you to carry it alone.

This week's verse reminds us that Jesus sees our burdens and invites us to give them to him. We may think crossing off our to-do lists will ease our anxiety, but true peace comes from surrendering what we're carrying to him. Anyone can give you productivity tips, but only Jesus offers rest for your soul. Because of Christ, your security comes from knowing that you are deeply loved and valued by God, no matter how much or how little you accomplish.

Come to me, all you who are weary and burdened, and I will give you rest. Take my yoke upon you and learn from me, for I am gentle and humble in heart, and you will find rest for your souls.

MATTHEW 11: 28–29

Ask God, "What do you want me to focus on today?" Then, listen to him instead of the world's pressures. God is a good Father. He doesn't want us to be overworked and drained—he simply asks us to be faithful, good stewards of the gifts and opportunities he's given us.

It's hard to take our eyes off of our to-do list, especially when it seems never-ending. But when we lift our eyes to focus on God and his desires for us, we receive rest for our souls. God's rest removes the pressures and worries that don't come from him and replaces them with his peace—a peace that can live in our hearts no matter how busy we are.

1. What is the biggest source of stress in your life right now? Have you talked to God about it?
2. What do you think "rest for your soul" would look like? How can you invite Jesus into your daily routine to experience it?
3. How often do you compare yourself to others? How does it affect your ability to feel peace?
4. Are you trying hard to prove yourself in an area of your life? What would it look like to rest in what God says about you?
5. How can you remind yourself that your worth isn't tied to your accomplishments? Is there a Scripture you love that can help when you feel overwhelmed?

PRAYER God, sometimes everything just feels like too much, no matter how hard I work. I'm so grateful that you see everything I'm carrying and that you care deeply for me. Please help me surrender my burdens to you and trust you to give me the peace in my heart that I desperately need.

Contentment in God's provision helps me fight envy.

A heart at peace gives life to the body, but envy rots the bones.

PROVERBS 14:30

Have you ever felt the sting of envy when visiting a friend's home, or as you scroll through pictures of someone showing off the latest gadget or fashion trend?

As a teen, I desperately wanted name-brand clothes, but they were out of reach for my family. One year, I begged my mom to drive me to an outlet mall for back-to-school shopping, but the prices were still too high. On the long drive home that evening, I felt heartbroken. Looking back, I wish I'd known then what I know now: that material things are just a tiny (and fleeting) part of a joyful, fulfilling life.

Trust me, I know that it's still disappointing. It still feels unfair. But here's the thing: envy won't make you feel any better. In fact, this week's verse says that envy rots our bones—a perfect description of how it poisons our hearts with bitterness. It's more than just wishing you had something—it's not being satisfied with what you do have and feeling bitter toward God or those who have it.

Even when my circumstances feel unfair, I don't want to waste my time wishing I had someone else's life—I want to fully embrace the beautiful life he's given me. God has promised to supply all my needs (Philippians 4:19) and hears my every prayer.

Why should I miss out on all the joys he's given me because my eyes are focused on someone else's blessings?

This week's verse shows us that peace is the antidote to envy. When we're content and at peace with all God has given us, trusting that he knows our needs and promises to fulfill them, we're able to enjoy our many blessings—without envy making us bitter and stealing our joy.

God promises that when we draw near to him, he will fulfill every desire that's in his will (Psalm 37:4) and he'll work in our hearts to transform any desires that don't align with him. So keep pouring out your heart to God, and as you pray for the things you desire, ask him to replace envy with his perfect peace. He will bring you the joy and contentment that only he can provide.

1. Have you ever thought that material things would make you happier? What happened when you got them (or didn't)?
2. What feelings arise when you compare yourself to others who seem to have more? How do these feelings impact the way you interact with God and others?
3. What might help you focus on the good things God has placed in your life and to rely on his help when that's difficult?

PRAYER God, sometimes I struggle with wanting what others have instead of focusing on the things you've blessed me with. It's hard to feel at peace when life seems unfair. I need your perspective to replace my own. Open my eyes to see that everything I have is a gift from you and that your presence in my life is all I need to experience true peace. Help me to live a life of gratitude and awareness of all my blessings.

I need God's help to guard my heart from the downsides of social media.

Above all else, guard your heart, for everything you do flows from it.

PROVERBS 4:23

Social media brings so much joy to my life and keeps me updated on issues I care about. But I'll be honest: it can also be a joy-stealer, tempting me to compare my life to others or question my worth. On top of that, it often robs me of precious time and peace of mind.

It's hard to separate the negative effects from the benefits of social media, and taking a break or setting limits can make us feel like we'll miss out on something. But you don't have to buy into the story social media tries to sell you—the one that values appearances over authenticity, pushes consumerism, and keeps you endlessly scrolling. You have the power to make choices that protect your heart, mind, and spirit.

How do we do this? The Bible says, "Guard your heart." Start by paying attention to the content you consume. If a post makes you feel envious or insecure, it's okay to unfollow, mute, or take a break. Follow accounts that inspire and uplift you and that point you closer to God.

It's also important to guard your time. Social media is designed to keep you scrolling, but *you* should control your time—not an algorithm. Set boundaries, like putting your phone away at a specific time of day or using app timers to help you stay present with the people around you.

Finally, reflect on why you're posting. Self-expression is fun, but consider whether you would feel as good about yourself if your post gets one like or 100. Do you love your image with and without a filter? Be honest about how social media makes you feel, and ask God to help you find your value in him, rather than online affirmations.

Keep asking God for guidance—he'll help you navigate it all.

1. How do you feel after spending time on social media? Are there patterns you've noticed?
2. How much time do you spend on social media each day? How could you set healthier boundaries to protect your time and focus?
3. When you post on social media, what motivates you? Are you seeking connection, validation, or something else?
4. Have you ever felt pressure to present a version of yourself on social media that isn't authentic? How can you align your online presence more with the real you?
5. Who in your life can help hold you accountable to make healthy decisions for your heart and mind as you use social media?

PRAYER   God, I need your help to keep my heart and mind healthy and at peace when I use social media. Help me to use my time wisely, recognizing the lies and giving me the strength to operate in your truth and your values so I can draw closer to you.

Living for God's approval releases me from people-pleasing.

If Paul's goal was to be liked, he'd be fighting an uphill battle. Christians judged him for his violent past of persecuting believers. Jews condemned him for preaching that salvation comes through faith in Jesus, not through following every Old Testament custom. And in the context of this week's verse, he's being accused of telling people what they want to hear. Criticized from all sides, Paul's response was clear: I'm living for God's approval, not theirs.

Let's be honest: most of us care what people think of us—we want to be liked. But when being "likeable" becomes our main goal, it pulls us away from God's purpose for our lives. Imagine if Paul had tried to please everyone: the Christians who judged his past, the Jews who rejected his message, and the Gentiles who didn't understand God's law. How could he possibly satisfy them all? Instead, Paul focused on pleasing God. That's what gave him the clarity and courage to persevere despite criticism.

I won't tell you to just "stop caring" what people think. Whether we show it on the outside or not, we all long to be appreciated for who we are. But don't

Am I now trying to win the approval of human beings or of God? Or am I trying to please people? If I were still trying to please people, I would not be a servant of Christ.

GALATIANS 1:10

miss that last part—for *who we are*. Being truly loved and accepted can't come from reshaping yourself to meet others' expectations. While trying to please everyone may get you approval, you'll lose sight of who you are and your unique God-given purpose in the process.

In high school, my classmates loved debating which rapper was the best. I never joined in, not because I didn't have an opinion but because I was afraid of choosing the "wrong" one and being judged. But one day, I noticed something. Everyone else shared their opinions freely, even when others disagreed. They weren't worried about saying the "right" thing; they just liked who they liked.

It may seem like a small thing, but in that moment, I saw how much my need for others' approval was silencing me and stopping me from being my true self.

Like Paul, we're called to live for only one person's approval: God's. The more we focus on what he says about us, the more we'll feel the freedom to show up as our full selves.

1. Are there areas of your life where you feel pressured to please others more than God?
2. Have you ever held back your true thoughts or beliefs because you were worried about how others would react?
3. How does God's unconditional love help free you from the need for other people's approval?
4. Who in your life encourages you to value God's approval and live authentically, in line with his values? How can you lean into those relationships more?

5. What would change in your daily life if you truly lived for God's approval above all else?
6. When have you felt the most confident and free to be yourself? Take some time to pray and ask God to help you feel that way more often.

PRAYER God, I need your help to value what you say is important. Help me to focus on living for you instead of becoming consumed by what others think of me. When I long for love and acceptance, remind me that true friends will embrace me for all of who you've called me to be and won't belittle my desire to live for you. Thank you for Paul's example of what it looks like to live out your mission on this earth and to honor you above everything else.

The sufficiency of Jesus frees me from perfectionism.

Whatever you do, work at it with all your heart, as working for the Lord, not for human masters.

COLOSSIANS 3:23

When something is important to us, we give it our best effort. But this week's verse reminds us who we're working for. Without this perspective, working hard at sports, academics, art, or even being a good friend can morph into perfectionism, which ignores God's grace and steals our joy.

Perfectionism might look like trying your best, but it's often driven by fear of disappointing others, appearing vulnerable, or failing. But disappointment, vulnerability, and failure are all a part of life. The harder we try to run from them by trusting in our own efforts, the further we drift from God's grace—a free gift that can't be earned.

Think about it: the only person who ever lived a perfect life was Jesus. Because we're "hidden in Christ" (Colossians 3:3), when God looks at us, he sees our perfect Savior! God already embraces and accepts you completely, not because of anything you've done but because of Jesus' perfection.

Your salvation frees you to work wholeheartedly, not for yourself or others but for the Lord. You don't need to strive for acceptance or approval—that's already secured! Instead, your efforts can flow from the unconditional love you've received from God and your desire to honor him.

When we rest in God's grace, a bad grade or missed opportunity doesn't define our worth. I had a friend who dreamed of attending a big university. She was devastated when she realized she'd have to live at home and attend community college because of limited finances. She felt embarrassed that she'd "failed" to achieve her dream.

But looking back, she sees God's grace. She met Jesus and made lasting friendships during community college. Later, she was able to transfer to a university, graduate with no debt, and embark on an incredibly fulfilling career. My friend learned that her worth wasn't based on taking the "perfect" path.

When you're tempted to trust your own efforts and plans, God invites you to lay your fears at his feet and trust that his grace will cover every mistake and disappointment.

1. When do you feel the most pressure to be "perfect"?
2. Do you struggle with the fear of disappointing others, appearing vulnerable, or failing? When does this fear show up for you?
3. How does knowing you are "hidden in Christ" change the way you see your mistakes or weaknesses?
4. What would it look like to glorify God in your efforts without striving for perfectionism?

PRAYER God, sometimes I feel pressure to be perfect, and I fear disappointing others or myself. Remind me of your grace to live in the freedom you've given me. Thank you that I'm "hidden in Christ" because of his death and resurrection. Please help me to keep the truth of the gospel at the center of all I do.

WEEK 21

Our bodies are God's creation and deserve honor, not criticism.

For you created my inmost being; you knit me together in my mother's womb. I praise you because I am fearfully and wonderfully made; your works are wonderful, I know that full well.

PSALM 139:13–14

When did we learn to be so critical of our bodies? I vividly remember the first time I felt ashamed of my body. I was enjoying a movie night with my friends when I glanced down, noticed my thighs, and hated the way they looked.

I didn't realize it then, but I was absorbing messages from the world around me. My mom was caught up in diet culture, and watching her strive to change her body (which, I realized, was built a lot like mine) left me believing that our bodies weren't "good."

Every day, we're bombarded with messages that contradict God's truth. Companies exploit our insecurities to make a profit, and social media algorithms push the lie that we need to fix or hide our bodies.

But God's Word says something entirely different. We are "fearfully and wonderfully made." He crafted us with such intricate care that we should stand in awe of his work—not despise it!

When we're being sold lies, how do we embrace God's truth? We can rewrite the narrative: when lies creep in, replace them with truth from God's Word.

Speak life over yourself and your friends, and interrupt negative body talk from others with kindness and grace.

You are God's masterpiece. Hear what he says about you, and choose to believe it—for yourself and those around you.

1. How does knowing that God "knit you together" and calls you "wonderfully made" change the way you view your body?
2. What messages about your body are you absorbing from the world? How do they compare to what God says about you?
3. What are some quick phrases you can use to interrupt negative body talk from friends or family? ("Sorry, we're body positive around here!" is a lighthearted one that always works for me.)
4. How can you replace shame-driven thoughts about eating or exercise with joy and gratitude for what your body can do?

PRAYER God, thank You for crafting me beautifully and intentionally. I'm grateful for the body you gave me and everything it can do. Sometimes, the messages from society make it hard to see my body through your eyes. When I'm feeling critical of my body, please flood my heart with your truth and help me to guard against the world's lies.

NOTE: If you or someone you know is constantly worried about their weight, food choices, or appearance in a way that's affecting their health and happiness, compassionate help is available. Visit allianceforeatingdisorders .com or call their helpline at 1-866-662-1235 to get connected to resources.

> *You keep track of all my sorrows. You have collected all my tears in your bottle. You have recorded each one in your book.*
>
> **PSALM 56:8 (NLT)**

Even when it feels like no one else can handle my emotions, God can.

Big emotions can be overwhelming. Sadness, anger, fear, or frustration can feel so intense that it seems like they'll never go away.

When my parents got divorced, I wasn't sure how to deal with the thunderstorm of emotions inside me. Sometimes, they exploded into anger, but I often pushed them down or hid them. Since I didn't really know how to speak about or process my feelings, I thought I should just try to move on, like it wasn't a big deal.

Big emotions are a normal part of being human, but most of us—at every age—are still learning how to handle them. Maybe you've tried to open up about your feelings, but you weren't met with empathy, or you were given a "solution" to your problem without really feeling heard first.

I've been there, and it's lonely to feel like no one can truly hold space for our emotions. But the good news is: God can. This week's verse reminds us that God knows our sorrows and that every emotion we feel matters to him. He is the ultimate safe space for our emotions because he never judges or glosses over how we're feeling. Instead, he listens with perfect love and understanding, providing a peace that no human can.

So, next time your emotions feel overwhelming, don't push them away. Take a deep breath and talk to God. With him, you can fully express yourself without fear of being judged or misunderstood.

And when you trust God with your emotions, he can help you learn to trust others with them, too. Experiencing God's perfect love and comfort can help us give more grace to our loved ones and embrace their imperfect efforts to support and console us. Our loved ones may not fully understand, but they can listen, pray for us, and remind us to run to our Heavenly Father, who knows each of his children completely.

1. How do you usually handle big emotions? Do you push them down, or do they tend to explode? How do you feel after?
2. Are there emotions that you've been hiding from God or others? Why do you think that is?
3. What would it look like to trust God as a safe space for your emotions? Take some time in prayer this week to open up to him in a new way.
4. Who in your life could you invite to become a safe person to talk to about your feelings?

PRAYER God, it's painful when I don't feel seen or understood by anyone in my life. Sometimes, my emotions feel too heavy to carry on my own. Please show me how real you truly are—that you really hear me and that you're a loving Father who wants to listen and help me process all the complex emotions in my heart.

When Pharaoh's horses, chariots and horsemen went into the sea, the LORD brought the waters of the sea back over them, but the Israelites walked through the sea on dry ground. Then Miriam the prophet, Aaron's sister, took a timbrel in her hand, and all the women followed her, with timbrels and dancing. Miriam sang to them:
"Sing to the LORD, for he is highly exalted. Both horse and driver he has hurled into the sea."

EXODUS 15:19–21

When I face challenges, God gives me courage.

My best friend is the bravest person I know. Shortly after college, she packed up her life and moved across the world to become a foster parent to six young girls. It was a complete leap of faith, but God gave her a vision, the courage to pursue it, and strength for every difficult moment. Her family grew from six daughters to 12, now all healthy adults, thriving because of her brave "yes" to God.

Her story reminds me of the courageous woman from this week's Scripture: Moses' big sister, Miriam. When Moses was born, the Israelites were enslaved under a cruel pharaoh who had ordered the death of every Hebrew baby boy. To save him, Moses' mother placed him in a basket on the Nile River.

Miriam walked along the river, keeping a close eye on her brother until she saw Pharaoh's daughter discover the basket. With courage and wisdom, Miriam offered to bring their mother to care for Moses, ensuring his survival and connection to his family.

Miriam's faith turned a desperate situation into a life-changing outcome. God strengthened her with courage to act decisively. Her story, and my best friend's, reminds us that God can steady our fearful hearts and guide us with his wisdom in challenging moments.

Decades later, in this week's verse, Miriam experienced another incredible miracle: the parting of the Red Sea, where God delivered the Israelites from slavery through Moses' leadership.

When they reached the other side, Miriam led the crowd in a celebratory song, directing the Israelites to give all the glory to God. Miriam recalled all the ways God had moved, from her childhood to her role now as a prophet and worship leader. She praised God for his faithfulness and invited her community to do the same.

Miriam's life shows us the power of a life rooted in faith. Her faith empowered her to lead by example, taking bold and confident steps for God's glory and for the good of his people.

1. What does Miriam's song teach you about giving credit to God during moments of victory?
2. Miriam's actions impacted her family and her community. How can your faith influence those around you?
3. Miriam had to overcome fear to act boldly. What fears might be holding you back from stepping into God's plan? How can you see yourself as part of God's bigger story?

PRAYER God, thank you for always having a greater plan in mind, even when I can't see it at first. It's amazing how you weave circumstances together for our good and for your glory. Please give me courage when things are difficult, and open my eyes to how I can glorify you in every circumstance.

PART THREE

Relating to Others

True friends help each other grow.

> *As iron sharpens iron, so one person sharpens another.*
>
> **PROVERBS 27:17**

Friendship is one of God's most precious gifts to us. Good friends love us for who we are *and* challenge us to grow, even when it's difficult. Through our friendships, God brings us not only comfort and companionship but teaching and transformation.

The day before auditions for my school musical, I was distraught. All afternoon, our dance instructor had been teaching us the audition piece, but I was completely lost. I felt embarrassed and defeated.

I loved singing and acting, and I dreamed of performing in all eight plays and musicals of my high school career—a rare achievement that was always celebrated at graduation. But there was no way I'd be ready to step on the stage to audition tomorrow, so I was ready to throw that dream away.

I swallowed back tears as I walked out of the auditorium with my best friend.

"Come home with me," she said. "We'll keep working on it."

And we did. All evening, she patiently coached me through the steps, over and over. We kept going until my anxiety was eclipsed by a peaceful confidence. I wouldn't be the best on the stage, but I had it together enough to make the cut.

I had been so discouraged that I almost gave up on something deeply important to me. Thankfully, my best friend knew that this experience could teach me a new level of perseverance. I still look back on that day as a reminder of what it looks like to persist through difficulty.

God calls us to "sharpen" each other, to remind each other of who we are in Christ when we're feeling defeated, and to encourage each other to live out the values that God has placed inside us, even when it's difficult.

1. Notice how your friends make you feel. Do you feel like they truly see and respect your desire to walk with Christ and live out his values? Have they ever encouraged you to do something that goes against who you are in Christ? Take some time to think about whether they value your growth and your walk with God, or if they have their own agenda for who they think you should be.

2. What are some ways you can tell that a friend truly brings out the best in you and wants the best for you? List a few examples from your own life.

3. Think of a close friend. Have you taken time to encourage and "sharpen" them lately? This week, listen to something that's important to them and ask how you can support them.

PRAYER God, help me to be a friend who encourages and "sharpens" the people I love. Help me find friends who encourage me to walk in your values and who support me as I grow more and more into the person you've called me to be.

> *One who has unreliable friends soon comes to ruin, but there is a friend who sticks closer than a brother.*
>
> **PROVERBS 18:24**

God helps me value what's important in friendships.

To celebrate my 17th birthday, I reserved a big table at my favorite restaurant and invited friends from all my social circles.

By the time dinner started, only six of us were there—laughing and enjoying the night but surrounded by empty chairs. When the waitress asked, "When is the rest of your party arriving?" I felt embarrassed and disappointed.

At the time, I thought being loved meant being surrounded by as many people as possible; the longer my list of friends, the less lonely my heart would feel. I wish I understood then what I finally do now—being surrounded by a crowd can never replace being truly seen, known, and loved, even by just a few.

Looking back, the friends who showed up that night were the ones who mattered most—friends who are still part of my life two decades later.

Longing for friendship is natural; God designed us to need one another. But *what* we value in our friendships matters. This week's verse reminds us that it's not about how many people surround us; it's about the depth of the connections we build. A small circle of loyal friends who truly know you, love you, and want to grow with you is far more valuable than a long list of surface-level friendships.

It doesn't matter how many seats you can fill at a birthday dinner. Do you have someone to call when life feels overwhelming? Someone who cheers for your victories louder than you do? Someone who speaks truth into your life (even when it's hard) because they know you deeply and want God's best for you? That's the kind of friend "who sticks closer than a brother."

And if you're still waiting to find that kind of connection, know this: you're never alone. Jesus is the ultimate friend who knows you fully and loves you deeply. Ask him to bring a good friend into your life, and allow him to walk with you as you wait, filling the empty spaces that only he can with his unchanging love.

1. What does true friendship mean to you? How is it different from having many acquaintances?
2. Have you ever felt like the number of friends you have defines your value? How does this week's verse challenge that idea?
3. What qualities do you look for in a friend? Are you reflecting those same qualities in your friendships? If not, how could you become a better friend?
4. Is there a friend in your life who's been loyal and supportive who you may have been taking for granted? How can you show appreciation for them?
5. What does it mean to you that Jesus is a friend "who sticks closer than a brother"? How can you lean on him in times of loneliness?

PRAYER God, I long for friendships where I'm truly known and deeply loved, but sometimes I value the wrong things in a friendship. Help me to appreciate the true connections I have in my life and to nurture their growth. If I have any wrong priorities, give me wisdom to see them and replace them with what you value.

God can use me to plant seeds of faith in the lives of my friends.

How should we talk to our friends who aren't Christians?

It can feel discouraging when people we care about don't believe in Jesus. We know how much our faith anchors us, and we want to share that hope with others, but the message doesn't always click right away.

I'll never forget a high school friend who lived her faith boldly. Even in hard times, she was kind, joyful, and unshakable in her faith in Jesus, and that made her stand out. Years later, I told her how much her example inspired me. She was blown away—she had no idea she'd left such a powerful impression!

In this week's verse, Paul reminds us of our role in spreading the gospel. We can plant or water seeds of faith, but the result isn't up to us. Only God can make those seeds grow.

How do we plant seeds? Share the gospel in your own words. When your friend is curious about why you pray or go to church, explain why you're grateful for a God who saved you and who strengthens you through life's ups and downs.

How do we water seeds? Whether or not those initial conversations seem to make an impact,

I planted the seed, Apollos watered it, but God has been making it grow. So neither the one who plants nor the one who waters is anything, but only God, who makes things grow. The one who plants and the one who waters have one purpose, and they will each be rewarded according to their own labor. For we are co-workers in God's service.

1 CORINTHIANS 3:6–9A

keep living out your faith authentically. Be kind, patient, and gentle—showing the fruits of the Spirit. Share God's work in your life in ways that come naturally; mention a Scripture that has encouraged you recently, or give God credit for the good he does in your life.

As you plant and water, pray for God to make those seeds grow in his perfect timing. Remember that sometimes, the seeds you plant won't grow until years later.

How you live your life matters. Even when you don't see it, God is working through you to reach others with his love.

1. Have you ever tried to share your faith with a friend? How did it go?
2. What holds you back from talking about Jesus with your friends?
3. Have you ever gotten frustrated when God's timing doesn't seem to match yours?
4. Do you think your friends see God through the way you live your life? Why or why not?
5. Can you think of someone whose faith has encouraged you? Is there something from their example that you can follow to show God's love to your friends?

PRAYER God, I'm so grateful for the friends you've placed in my life. Help me to trust your timing in how you choose to reveal yourself to them. I trust that we're in each other's lives for a reason, and I pray that you will help me plant and water seeds of faith that you will make grow in your perfect timing.

No one is too far from God to be saved.

When I was a new believer, my excitement for living for God unintentionally turned into judgment toward others who didn't live the way I thought they should. Without realizing it, I started sorting people into categories: "real" Christians—those who avoided outward, "obvious" sins—and others who seemed more "worldly." Among non-Christians, I saw some as more likely to come to Christ and others as "too far gone."

At that time, Rahab would have landed on my "too far gone" list because of her profession. But her story in the book of Joshua reminds us to never judge by outward appearances and never underestimate what God can do in someone's heart.

Rahab lived in Jericho, a city doomed for destruction. When she heard about God parting the Red Sea and giving the Israelites victory over their enemies, she realized that he must be the one true God of heaven and earth (Joshua 2:11). So when two Israelite spies came to Jericho, Rahab risked her life to hide them from the authorities. In exchange, she asked for a guarantee of her family's safety— that's how convinced she was that God would give the Israelites victory.

Then they burned the whole city and everything in it, but they put the silver and gold and the articles of bronze and iron into the treasury of the LORD's house. But Joshua spared Rahab the prostitute, with her family and all who belonged to her, because she hid the men Joshua had sent as spies to Jericho—and she lives among the Israelites to this day.

JOSHUA 6:24–25

Rahab's faith was extraordinary, so much so that she is honored in Hebrews 11 alongside Abraham, Isaac, Jacob, and other heroes of the faith. She later married an Israelite and is even listed in Jesus' lineage as King David's great-grandmother (Matthew 1:5)!

Looking back, it pains me to realize that my younger self would have written Rahab off completely. Thankfully, God is patient with us when we're judgmental. Now, when I'm tempted to label certain people or public figures as "hopeless," I'm reminded that God alone has the final say. Rahab's story encourages us to let love and hope lead instead of judgment and to believe that God can transform lives in ways we could never imagine.

1. Have you ever been tempted to label someone as "too far gone"? How can Rahab's example shift your thinking?
2. Think about a time when you judged someone based on outward appearances or their past. How might you think about them differently now?
3. Rahab's faith led her to take courageous action. Is there an area of your life where you feel God calling you to step out in faith?
4. In what ways have you seen God transform someone's life, either in Scripture, history, or in your own experience?

PRAYER God, you are the only one who can see our hearts. Thank you that no one is ever too far from you to be saved and for giving us Rahab's powerful example of faith in action. When I'm tempted to judge someone, remind me that you are the only one who sees the heart. Help me to lead with love instead.

WEEK 28

God can help me speak in a way that honors him and communicates his love.

Words stick. They're easy to say but impossible to take back. In the moment, speaking my mind can feel satisfying, but that feeling fades fast. I once shared what I thought was constructive criticism with a coworker, but I hadn't thought about how to present it kindly. The moment her face fell, I realized I should have chosen my words more carefully. My thoughtless remark caused unnecessary hurt, and I felt instant regret.

This week's verse challenges us to choose words that are wholesome and helpful. Like a nutritious meal that brings nutrients and benefits to our bodies, our words should leave people better off than they were before: encouraged, supported, and built up.

That might sound like a high standard, but with the Holy Spirit's help, it's possible. Here's one practical tool: before speaking, pause and ask yourself these three questions:

- ★ *Is it true?*
- ★ *Is it helpful?*
- ★ *Is it kind?*

Do not let any unwholesome talk come out of your mouths, but only what is helpful for building others up according to their needs, that it may benefit those who listen.

EPHESIANS 4:29

Our words are powerful; they can build others up or tear them down. Sometimes, we speak harshly without realizing it, thinking out loud without considering the impact of our words. Other times, we're driven by strong emotions and speak out of frustration, without caring how it affects the other person. But both of these situations have the same root: putting our own feelings above someone else's.

When a subject is sensitive or emotions are running high, pausing before you speak can protect your relationships and save you from years of regret. Most importantly, it's an opportunity to reflect God's kindness and love to the people in your life.

1. Think about a time when someone's words had a big impact on you. Were they encouraging or hurtful? How did you feel?

2. Have you ever said something you regretted? How did it impact your relationship? What would you have done differently?

3. What situations make it hardest for you to pause before speaking? How can you invite God into those moments to help you reflect his character when you respond?

4. Do you lean more toward speaking your mind without pausing to think or holding back when you should speak up? How can this week's verse help you find the right balance?

PRAYER God, I want to honor you in the way I speak to others. Please help me to pause before I speak and choose words that reflect your heart. Help my speech to be wholesome—building up the people around me with encouragement and support. Even when I have to share a difficult truth, help me to do so with grace and love.

Everyone—even people I find hard to love—is made in the image of God.

Loving people isn't always easy. It's not hard to love your best friend, but what about the girl who spreads rumors about you or the guy who makes rude comments every time you walk by? What about the person everyone else ignores?

You all have one thing in common: you're all made in God's image (Genesis 1:27), and that truth changes everything. When we see everyone as God's image-bearers, it challenges us to rethink how we see and treat them.

I have a friend who I never thought I'd get close to. I'm loud and boisterous, while she's reflective and soft-spoken. She's not quick to speak up in group settings, but when I finally talked to her one-on-one, I realized how kind, thoughtful, and wise she is! I'm so glad God gave me the chance to rethink my assumptions, because I would have missed out on a wonderful friendship.

God's love is unconditional. We're called to reflect his love to others, whether or not we think they "deserve" it. Liking someone is optional, but

We love because he first loved us. Whoever claims to love God yet hates a brother or sister is a liar. For whoever does not love their brother and sister, whom they have seen, cannot love God, whom they have not seen.

1 JOHN 4:19–20

treating them with love and dignity is something that God calls us to do no matter what.

This perspective also helps us reconsider our assumptions. Maybe that "weird" kid is interesting and hilarious once you take the time to talk to them. Loving others doesn't mean being best friends with everyone, but it does mean treating them with dignity and kindness as God's image-bearers.

When we understand how deeply God loves us—flaws, mistakes, and all—it softens our hearts toward those who mistreat us or people we just don't seem to "click" with. Of course, this doesn't mean we agree with hurtful actions or tolerate mistreatment. Instead, it empowers us to choose love, no matter how others act.

The next time you're tempted to snap at someone who's rude or ignore someone who seems "different," pause and ask God to help you see them through his eyes. Pray for them, even if it's hard. You never know how your act of love could impact their heart—or yours.

1. Can you think of a time when you judged someone without really knowing them? How might seeing them as God's image-bearer have changed your perspective?

2. Why do you think it's easier to love some people than others? How can God help us through this?

3. How does understanding God's unconditional love for you help you love others better?

4. Have you ever experienced kindness from someone you least expected? How did that impact you?

5. When someone mistreats you, what steps can you take to respond with love instead of frustration?

6. In what ways can showing love to someone who feels ignored or "different" reflect God's heart?

PRAYER God, please help me see the people around me through your eyes instead of my own. When I'm tempted to make assumptions about someone, remind me to pray for them instead. Please give me wisdom and strength to live as a representation of your love and to treat everyone with dignity simply because you made them in your image.

God's forgiveness empowers us to forgive others.

> Be kind and compassionate to one another, forgiving each other, just as in Christ God forgave you.
>
> **EPHESIANS 4:32**

As a teen, I was deeply hurt by two close family members. We didn't speak for years, and their absence left a painful void at birthdays, prom, and college move-in day—so many milestones missed. Even when we began talking again, I held onto bitterness, waiting for an apology that never came. But one day, God used my husband's words to open my eyes.

My husband shared this truth with me: Jesus didn't die just for my sins but for everyone who believes in him—even those who hurt me. If God had already forgiven them, who was I to hold on to bitterness? Did I really have more of a right to be offended than God?

Jesus modeled that forgiveness is a choice—he didn't wait for our apology before he forgave us, and he asks us to do the same. So, even though the pain of the past was still real, I chose to forgive.

Once I decided to forgive, miraculously, God's love flooded into the places that used to hold only pain and bitterness. When I heard just a few weeks later that this family member was very sick, my heart genuinely broke for them—such a strange feeling after so many years of bitterness! I reached out to encourage them, which led to a warm, healing conversation—and, unexpectedly, their first apology. It was clear this was God's work.

Forgiving didn't erase the hurt, but it did something even more powerful: it transformed my own heart. It helped me understand God's forgiveness more fully and allowed me to finally see the other person through his eyes—flawed and complex, yet deeply loved and completely forgiven. Forgiveness doesn't change the past, but it does change us—freeing our hearts to love the way God loves and to walk in his healing.

1. Is there a situation in your life where you're holding onto hurt or bitterness? What would it look like to forgive, even if they never apologize?

2. Forgiveness doesn't erase the pain, but it can change your heart. Why do you think forgiving others can lead to God doing such transformative work in our hearts, like in this week's story?

3. What does it mean to forgive someone in your heart, without necessarily confronting them? How could that be a first step toward healing?

4. How does it feel to remember that God sees the people who have hurt you with love and compassion, just as he sees you? How can this change your perspective?

PRAYER   God, thank you for forgiving me completely when you sent Jesus to die for my sins. Help me see that your cross has the power to heal my relationship not only with you but also with those who've hurt me. Help me trust you with the pain I've experienced, and open my eyes to see those who've hurt me through your eyes, as your beloved children.

Do nothing out of selfish ambition or vain conceit. Rather, in humility value others above yourselves, not looking to your own interests but each of you to the interests of the others. In your relationships with one another, have the same mindset as Christ Jesus: [. . .] And being found in appearance as a man, he humbled himself by becoming obedient to death—even death on a cross!

PHILIPPIANS 2:3-5, 8

WEEK 31

When we humble ourselves and apologize, we reflect Jesus' selfless character.

You'd probably never guess that I once bullied someone. But in elementary school, I once turned my whole class against an innocent classmate. I'll never forget the pain in my classmate's eyes before she covered her face, trying to hold back sobs. Suddenly my prank didn't feel funny anymore; it broke me inside to know that her pain was all my fault. But instead of apologizing, I hurried off to my desk, grateful my teacher didn't know who was responsible.

At the time, my biggest concern was not getting caught. I should have put my classmate's interests first, humbled myself, and taken responsibility for my actions. Instead, I prioritized my own comfort and never even apologized.

Recently, I saw a similar scene in a movie. But in this movie, you can see on the bully's face that the weight of her mistake has transformed her. She didn't just feel bad; she apologized and completely changed, even putting her reputation on the line to make things right.

The Bible calls this repentance. The original Greek word means more than feeling regret; it's a total redirection away from sin and toward God. True repentance requires deep humility—that's what makes it so powerful.

In this week's verse, Paul points to Jesus as our ultimate example. If Jesus—who did no wrong—could humble himself for our sake, how much more should we be willing to humble ourselves for others?

So how can we put our pride aside and apologize well? Admit your mistake and take ownership of your actions without excuses. It's also crucial to acknowledge the harm. Let the person know that you see how your actions impacted them. Finally, commit to change. Share how you plan to do better moving forward—and never hesitate to ask God for help in that.

1. Can you think of a time when you hurt someone and found it hard to apologize? What held you back?
2. How does Jesus' example of humility in Philippians 2 inspire you to approach your relationships differently?
3. Is there someone in your life right now you need to apologize to? What step can you take today to make it right?
4. How can you make sure your apologies aren't just words but also lead to real change in your behavior?

PRAYER God, thank you for modeling humility when you came to earth for my sake. I confess that I am often selfish and prideful instead of following your example. I need your help to humble myself, especially when my pride makes it hard to apologize. Transform my heart to look more like Jesus.

I need Christian community in order to grow.

And let us consider how we may spur one another on toward love and good deeds, not giving up meeting together, as some are in the habit of doing, but encouraging one another— and all the more as you see the Day approaching.

HEBREWS 10:24–25

When I read the phrase "spur one another on" in this week's verse, I immediately picture a sports team celebrating when a teammate scores or encouraging one another in the locker room after a tough game. Whether they're on the field, on the sidelines, or at practice, teammates constantly encourage, advise, and energize each other. Imagine how strange it would be if every player minded their own business during a game, staying silent when someone made a great play and avoiding giving advice in the locker room. That would never happen!

In the same way, Christianity is a team sport. If you read the book of Acts, you'll see that early Christians spent a LOT of time together. Prayer times often flowed into meal times, and believers leaned on each other to meet even their most basic needs.

Today, though, many of us live in societies that value independence so much that asking for help feels like admitting weakness. But God designed us to need each other, especially when it comes to growing in our faith.

On my faith journey, communities of fellow believers have supported me in countless ways. They've cried with me during moments of deep grief, shown up with meals when I needed comfort, prayed for me when I had no words to pray for myself, and challenged me to grow by asking hard questions. Although I've lived far from my biological family in many seasons of my life, I've always known who I could call in an emergency because of my family in Christ.

Do you have Christian sisters and brothers to rely on as you grow in your faith? Maybe there's a youth group, a church small group, or a Christian club you can join. But if there isn't, don't be discouraged; finding even one or two friends or mentors who share your faith can make all the difference. God's design for us is to walk together, encouraging one another and spurring each other on toward love and good deeds.

1. Who in your life has "spurred you on" in your faith journey? How can you thank them or encourage them in return?

2. Have you ever hesitated to ask for help or to share your struggles with others? What held you back, and how could you overcome that?

3. How does spending time with other believers impact your relationship with God?

4. If you don't have a strong Christian community yet, where do you think you could look for one?

5. Think of a fellow Christian in your life. How can you encourage them in their faith this week?

PRAYER God, I recognize that I can't do this Christian walk alone. I want to build loving, trusting relationships within a Christian community. Please help me open my heart and grow in trust so that I can invite true accountability and encouragement into my life.

Honor your father and your mother, so that you may live long in the land the LORD your God is giving you.

EXODUS 20:12

WEEK 33

When I honor my parents, I honor God.

What does it mean to honor your parents?

The Hebrew translation for "honor" is *kabed*, which means "weighty" in terms of importance. God uses this wording in the Ten Commandments to emphasize the significance of the parent–child relationship. Honoring your parents with obedience acknowledges the unique and vital role they play in your life—a role designed by God for your good.

This can be challenging, since parents exist on a wide spectrum. Some are Christians; some aren't. Some are loving and wise, while others may struggle to offer healthy guidance. But walking with Jesus means doing what he asks of us. We honor our parents, not because they have the perfect parenting resume but because we trust that God's commands are all for our ultimate good. (Read Psalm 19:7–11 for a beautiful reflection on this!)

When we align our hearts with God's commands, including honoring our parents, we reflect his love and faithfulness, which brings him glory. In this week's verse, God even attaches a promise to this commandment, a reminder that obedience to God leads to a life of peace and joy in him.

Of course, there are exceptions to consider. God never asks us to endure abuse or to follow someone into sin. But in most cases, honoring your parents means choosing respect, gratitude, and humility to reflect the character of God.

This week, practice honoring your parents in one of these ways:

* Find something you're grateful for and thank them for it.
* Pray for them, asking God to guide them with wisdom and grace.
* Be open to their advice and perspective, listening to understand even when you don't fully agree.
* Look for small ways to serve them or lighten their load in honor of the ways they've cared for you.

When God sees that our hearts desire to follow him, he deepens our intimacy with him and strengthens us when obedience feels difficult.

1. How does the word *honor* being related to the word *weighty* help you understand God's heart for parents and children more?
2. Are there ways you've struggled to honor your parents? How can you ask God for help in this area?
3. Read Psalm 19:7–11. How does focusing on the goodness of God's commands help you obey him?
4. Have you ever experienced a blessing from God as a result of obeying his commands, even when it was hard?

PRAYER God, I confess that sometimes the command to honor and obey can feel difficult. Please help me to see the beauty in your commands and help me to desire your glory more than my own comfort. When obedience is hard, remind me that ultimately, I'm loving and honoring you when I honor my parents.

Children, obey your parents in the Lord, for this is right. "Honor your father and mother"—which is the first commandment with a promise—"so that it may go well with you and that you may enjoy long life on the earth." Fathers, do not exasperate your children; instead, bring them up in the training and instruction of the Lord.

EPHESIANS 6:1–4

WEEK 34

I can communicate with love and respect for my parents, even when it's hard.

Honoring someone means recognizing their importance in your life and reflecting that in how you treat them. It looks like speaking kindly, assuming good intentions, and forgiving mistakes.

But let's be honest—this isn't always easy. As a teen, my parents often got the worst of my frustration, impatience, and big emotions. After long days filled with school, friendships, and activities, home was where I could let it all out. I wish I understood then that they deserved the same kindness and consideration I gave my friends and teachers—if not more. But ironically, the opposite was true.

Honoring your parents doesn't mean agreeing with everything they say or ignoring unhealthy behavior. It means recognizing their God-given role in your life and asking for God's help to respond with love, even when you're frustrated.

If you've never felt free to speak openly and honestly to your parents, you may wonder how to do so in a way that still honors them. A good place to start is to think about your relationship with God. When he calls you to obey him, he's not asking you to be a robot, following orders without emotion or thought. He invites you into a loving, honest relationship where you can pour your heart out to him, admit when obeying feels hard, and ask him for help.

In the same way, obedience to your parents should be built on a foundation of love and healthy communication. If you feel unheard or mistreated, it's important to address those issues—perhaps with the help of a trusted adult if the situation is serious.

Healthy relationships require effort from both sides. But even if things feel strained, you can still be faithful to God's command to honor your parents. One way to keep your heart soft is by remembering that they're human, too. It's easy to be consumed by our own lives and forget that our parents carry their own burdens and emotions. Taking a moment to see things from their perspective is a first step toward honoring them and ultimately, glorifying God.

1. How would you describe your family's communication styles? How could you contribute to a healthier dynamic?
2. Is there something you've been wanting to share with your parents? How could you express it in a respectful way?
3. Is there an adult in your life that you could ask for advice if you and your parents are struggling to understand each other?
4. How often do you pray for your parents? How could praying for them give you a new perspective about their role in your life?

PRAYER God, I want to have a relationship with my parents that's healthy and respectful. Please give us all wisdom on how to share honestly and lovingly with each other, even when it's hard. I trust that you will help us understand each other and give us grace to communicate with love.

Listen, my son, to your father's instruction and do not forsake your mother's teaching. They are a garland to grace your head and a chain to adorn your neck.

PROVERBS 1:8–9

As I grow in independence, I can still trust my parents for guidance.

As a teen, I was proud of my independence, relying on my own sense of right and wrong to guide my life. I closed off certain parts of my life from my parents, convinced I could handle everything on my own—especially when it came to friendships and romantic relationships.

I didn't know it at the time, but many of the challenges I faced were things that my mom had almost certainly been through, and talking to her would have made me feel less alone. At the time, my independence felt empowering, but looking back, I realize I missed out on something valuable: the wisdom and life experience of my parents.

Becoming more independent is a natural part of the season you're in, but you aren't meant to navigate it alone. God has given parents a unique responsibility for their children's well-being. Think about it: your parents are the only people on earth whose primary job is to guide, protect, and care for you. They've taken on a tremendous responsibility, and if they're Christians, they're likely praying for God's wisdom every step of the way. They aren't perfect and will make mistakes, but their role is one worth honoring.

It can be tempting to shut your parents out of your day-to-day life, especially when you're craving independence, but doing so is like leaving a valuable gift unopened. When you close yourself off from their guidance, you might miss out on the wisdom, comfort, and support that God intends to provide for you through them.

It's normal to get frustrated with your parents at times, especially if they seem a little too controlling or intrusive. Be honest with them about how you feel, but also remember that deep down, they probably have good intentions. They want what's best for you and are trying to help you stay on the right path. Finding ways to open up to them and then listening to their thoughts can create a healthier relationship for you both.

1. Do you view your independence as a strength? How might that impact your relationship with your parents?
2. Are there areas of your life you've kept hidden from your parents? How could involving them help you?
3. Have you ever asked your parents about their own life experiences and what they've learned from them? What's something you could ask them about this week?
4. What would it look like to trust that God is working through your parents to guide and support you?

PRAYER God, I don't want to miss any of the blessings that you want to provide through my parents. Thank you for choosing them as my parents. Please help me take one small step to open up to them in a new way and open my heart to their guidance.

> *Love is patient, love is kind. It does not envy, it does not boast, it is not proud. It does not dishonor others, it is not self-seeking, it is not easily angered, it keeps no record of wrongs. Love does not delight in evil but rejoices with the truth. It always protects, always trusts, always hopes, always perseveres.*
>
> **1 CORINTHIANS 13:4–7**

A romantic relationship should honor God and reflect his definition of love.

Love in all its forms, including romantic love, can be one of God's greatest gifts. But love is much deeper and more significant than a feeling of attraction or butterflies; it's a reflection of God's patience, kindness, humility, respect, forgiveness, and honesty.

Romantic relationships can bring joy and fulfillment, but only if they're centered on shared values rooted in Christ. A relationship should inspire us to deepen our relationship with God, not distract us from it. If you're considering getting into a relationship, or if you're already in one, here are some important things to consider:

* Do I currently have an active, growing relationship with God? Will this relationship draw me closer or pull me away from him?
* What are the rules and boundaries my parents have set for relationships? Am I honoring them?
* Am I confident in who I am as a child of God, or am I hoping that a relationship will make me feel better about myself?

* Can I communicate in a healthy way with this person? Do they respect my boundaries and values? Do I feel comfortable being my authentic self with them?
* Have I thought about my physical boundaries and how to communicate them clearly?
* Do I have trusted mentors or friends who I feel comfortable asking for guidance, prayer, and wisdom?

If you desire to be in a romantic relationship, take some time to ask God to guide you and show you ways in which he may want you to grow to be ready. And if you're already in a relationship, go through the questions above with a trusted friend, parent or guardian, or mentor to ensure your relationship reflects God's values.

One thing I wish I'd known about relationships as a teen is that balance is key. I was in a long-term relationship in high school that was mostly positive, but looking back, I regret letting it take so much time away from my friends, family, and hobbies. Love can make you want to spend every waking moment with someone, but, trust me, you don't want to neglect the other important relationships in your life. Spend time together in groups, and be intentional about nurturing *all* parts of your life, not just your relationship.

1. How does this week's Scripture challenge or affirm the way you think about love?
2. In what ways can you prioritize your relationship with God before entering into a romantic relationship?
3. What qualities do you believe are essential in a Christ-centered relationship?

4. Who are the mentors or trusted friends you can turn to for practical advice and wisdom?

PRAYER God, I thank you that you show me every day through your character what love truly looks like. I pray that you would give me discernment and wisdom when it comes to romantic relationships. Help me to consider what choice will draw me closer to you, instead of relying on my feelings to make a decision. Thank you for promising to give me guidance when I ask.

Understanding God's purpose for sex frees me from shame and helps me wait.

Sex is a topic loaded with emotions, opinions, and—for many of us—shame. As a teen, we didn't really discuss it at home. My mom brought it up once; I awkwardly dodged the question, and that was that. And at school, the conversations were confusing—sometimes it seemed like everyone was doing it, but the moment I was honest about my own experiences, I felt judged.

The truth is, God created sex for a beautiful purpose: to strengthen a married couple's emotional, physical, and spiritual bond for a healthy, lifelong marriage. But too often, the messages we get from both the church and the world about sex are clouded with shame. Instead of acknowledging that sexual desires are natural, God-given, and good (in the right context), we're often taught to be ashamed of them, which makes honest, healthy conversations even harder.

Let's be clear—experiencing sexual desire is part of how God made us. We all desire to feel fully seen, known, and loved, and God designed marriage to be one of the most significant ways to experience this (second only to our relationship with him). In

That is why a man leaves his father and mother and is united to his wife, and they become one flesh.
Adam and his wife were both naked, and they felt no shame.

GENESIS 2:24–25

a godly marriage, a couple experiences the intimacy of sex *only* with each other, making them feel safe, secure, and deeply loved.

God wants us to enjoy sex the way Adam and Eve did—without shame and full of trust, freedom, and vulnerability. This is only possible within the beautiful, lifelong commitment of marriage.

Sex is treated so casually in our world that choosing to wait might make you feel out of place. But remember: God honors your faith and trust in his design. A wise teen shared with me, "This may not be the last person you ever date, and if you do break up, it might hurt so much more if you've had sex." She's right. The emotional "glue" of sex, meant to bond marriages, can create baggage and pain that God wants to protect us from.

So how do you manage these desires in the meantime? First, rest in God's perfect love for you—only he can perfectly fulfill your desire to feel fully seen and known. Second, nurture friendships where you're fully embraced for who you are and encouraged to rely on God's grace.

And when physical desires feel overwhelming, take practical steps in the moment like pausing to pray, exercising to release physical tension, planning meaningful time with friends where you can share vulnerably, or journaling about your honest feelings. Having a trusted person in your life who you can call or text in the moment for prayer and support is also a powerful tool for accountability.

If you've sinned in this area, know that God's mercies are new every morning, and you don't need to carry shame. Ask for his forgiveness and make a decision to honor what God says about sex. Trust him to strengthen you against temptation and prepare you for the lifelong joy and emotional safety of sex the way he intended it.

1. How can you combat the pressure of the world's casual view of sex with God's truth?
2. Why do you think God designed sex to be within the safety of marriage? How can waiting to have sex protect your emotional and spiritual health, both now and in the future?
3. If you're currently in a relationship where you're having sex, who can you ask for help to realign your choices with God's values?
4. When you feel lonely or out of place for following God's standards, what truths or Bible verses can you cling to for encouragement?

PRAYER God, thank You for designing sex with such intentionality. Help me to see the beauty in your design, even when my own struggles and temptations make it hard to see. Please give me a fresh revelation of how deeply you know and love me, and strengthen me to fight temptation as I wait.

PART FOUR

Faith: Walking It Out

My age doesn't determine my value in God's Kingdom.

Our world often underestimates younger people. It can feel like society only values you if you have years of experience and accomplishments on your resume—that you'll only "understand" and be able to make an impact "when you're older."

In this week's passage, we meet a young girl named Rhoda. She worked as a servant in a home (probably a house church) where many Christians had gathered to pray for the apostle Peter's release from prison. Think about this—while the adults were still praying, Rhoda's faith allowed her to recognize the answer to their prayers before anyone else! As a servant, she may not have been allowed to pray with them, but she was clearly trusting that God would come through, and her heart was ready to witness a miracle.

Rhoda's story shows that your faith and significance aren't tied to your age. In God's kingdom, every person has equal value. From the moment you accept Jesus as your Lord and Savior, he equips you to live out your faith and make an impact right now, no matter how young you are.

I attended a small church where the children's ministry always needed volunteers. The church only had one teen, and she probably wished there were

Peter knocked at the outer entrance, and a servant named Rhoda came to answer the door. When she recognized Peter's voice, she was so overjoyed she ran back without opening it and exclaimed, "Peter is at the door!"
"You're out of your mind," they told her. When she kept insisting that it was so, they said, "It must be his angel." But Peter kept on knocking, and when they opened the door and saw him, they were astonished.

ACTS 12:13–16

others her age, but that didn't stop her from allowing God to use her. On her own, she offered to teach at children's church, even volunteering for extra tasks. She served out of a genuine love for God and for the children of the church at a time when her help was desperately needed. Her commitment, like Rhoda's faith, shows that God can use teens in powerful ways if you trust him and stay ready to join in what he's doing.

Although the world may underestimate you, don't let anyone look down on you because you're young (1 Timothy 4:12). Your age doesn't determine the size of your faith; in fact, it's often young people who have the courage to believe that God can do impossible things. The world may underestimate you, but God sees your unique gifts and potential. Trust that he will use you to inspire others and carry out his plans.

1. Why do you think young people often have the courage to believe in the "impossible" more easily than adults?
2. What are some ways you can set an example for others with your faith and actions, like Rhoda did?
3. Is there a situation in your life where you feel God is calling you to step up, even though others may underestimate you?
4. Like Rhoda, how can you stay ready to join in when God moves?

PRAYER God, I want to be an example of the faith, joy, and strength that come from a relationship with you. When I'm tempted to feel insignificant because of my age, remind me of how you've always used young people—like Rhoda—to display the power that comes from faith in you.

He has shown you, O mortal, what is good. And what does the LORD require of you? To act justly and to love mercy and to walk humbly with your God.

MICAH 6:8

When I'm mourning the state of the world, God can help me be his hands and feet.

As we mature, we start to see the world more clearly. Our eyes are opened to injustice and suffering, both in our own communities and across the globe. And when these issues impact groups we belong to or people we care about, the pain is magnified.

This awareness can be overwhelming. With so many problems in the world, how do we figure out which ones to focus on? How do we handle the sadness or fear that comes from what feels like a constant stream of bad news? And what can we do if the pain we see is right in our own neighborhoods?

Where I live, homelessness is a huge issue. I love witnessing all the ways people come together to make a difference. There's a local organization that cooks and hands out meals each week, another that distributes water, and another that assembles care packages. Other groups focus on local policies to provide more housing and health services. Whatever you're passionate about, and however you want to serve, there's probably someone doing meaningful work that you can partner with.

A wise friend once reminded me that lasting change almost always happens in community.

So if you're not sure where to start, look close to home. What are people already doing to serve others—at your church or in your neighborhood—and how can you join them?

When I feel discouraged by the state of the world, taking small steps to help brings hope to my heart. And serving alongside others reminds me of the beauty in being "God's hands and feet" wherever he has placed us.

As members of the body of Christ, God has created each of us uniquely—so it's okay if your passion looks different from your friends'. Maybe you care deeply about the environment while your best friend feels called to help tutor young kids. That's the beauty of being "many parts, one body" (1 Corinthians 12:12); there's room for all of us to make a difference in the way God is calling us to.

As you work for change, remember that the world won't be fully healed until Jesus comes back. Our efforts matter and make a difference in the lives of others, but they're just one small piece of God's plan. When Jesus returns, he'll put every single puzzle piece into place, and there will be no more tears, pain, or suffering. Until then, keep reflecting his love by serving those around you.

1. What issue in your community or in the world breaks your heart the most? Why?
2. What gifts has God uniquely given you to make a difference in that area?
3. How can your faith in Jesus help you stay motivated to serve, even when problems seem overwhelming?
4. Think of someone you know (either personally or in history) who has made a difference in their community. What encourages you about their example?
5. What is one small step you could take this week to serve others?

PRAYER God, sometimes I'm overwhelmed by the suffering I see in my community and in the world. Please show me how deeply you care about people in need and help me see ways that I can make a difference. Please keep my heart encouraged and remind me of the beauty of your kingdom that will one day come and end all suffering.

With God, I should always expect the unexpected.

"God, show me who you truly are."

I've been praying this a lot lately. At my church, God is moving in new, exciting ways that I didn't expect, and honestly, sometimes it throws me off. Is this really how God works?

When I first became a Christian at 19 years old, I was blown away that God loved me enough to save me. I was wide-eyed and openhearted, ready for anything he wanted to do. But over time, I fell into a routine. I began to assume I knew how God worked, and I stopped expecting him to show up in new ways.

Jesus' neighbors in Matthew 13 struggled with this too. They thought they knew everything about him: his family, his background, his job. They had put Jesus in a box, so when he started doing miracles and teaching with authority, they couldn't believe it. Instead of celebrating him, they rejected him because he didn't fit their expectations.

Maybe you can relate. Maybe you've grown up hearing about God in church or at home and feel pretty clear on how God works. Or maybe you've been walking with Jesus for a while and your faith feels routine instead of alive and vibrant.

Coming to his hometown, [Jesus] began teaching the people in their synagogue, and they were amazed. "Where did this man get this wisdom and these miraculous powers?" they asked. "Isn't this the carpenter's son? Isn't his mother's name Mary, and aren't his brothers James, Joseph, Simon and Judas? Aren't all his sisters with us? Where then did this man get all these things?" And they took offense at him.

MATTHEW 13:54–57

But here's the truth: God is always doing something new, and he's always bigger than we could ever imagine. If we think we have God all figured out, we might miss him when he shows up in unexpected ways. And I don't want to miss an encounter with God!

So here's my challenge to you: don't let your familiarity with God keep you from seeing his power. Don't put limits on what he can do in your life, your church, or the world around you. Keep praying, "God, show me who you truly are," and trust him to surprise you with his goodness.

1. Have you ever found yourself putting God in a "box" based on your own experiences or expectations?
2. How has your view of God changed since you first began your faith journey?
3. Are there any ways you doubt God's work because it doesn't fit your expectations?
4. What is one area of your life where you've stopped expecting God to show up? How can you invite him into that space this week?
5. Is there someone in your life whose relationship with God is a bit different than yours? Consider spending some time with them and letting their experiences with God expand how you see him.

PRAYER God, I'm so grateful to be learning more about you each day. I pray that you would keep showing me new facets of who you are. When I'm tempted to think I have you all figured out, I pray that you would surprise me with a new revelation of who you are and what you can do.

Every change my body experiences was orchestrated by God.

Yet you, LORD, are our Father. We are the clay, you are the potter; we are all the work of your hand.

ISAIAH 64:8

Your body is your home here on earth. That might sound a little strange, but it's a truth I wish I had understood more in seasons of big changes for my body.

Change is a natural part of life. You've probably changed schools, moved, or discovered a new favorite hobby. But changes in your body feel different since it's an essential part of who you are.

During puberty, your body can start to feel unfamiliar, like a stranger. You may not recognize it anymore. And when others comment on it or treat you differently because of it, it can make you feel even more self-conscious. My chest developed later than most of my friends, and my peers' insensitive comments made it hard for me to love and embrace my body.

But the thing is, you can't run away from your body. It'll be your home for as long as you live. So, what if you got to know it?

Think of this time as a journey where your mind, body, and soul are walking hand-in-hand, learning how to work together again. Be patient with yourself. The last time you changed this much, you were a baby! And this won't be the last time you'll need to relearn and reconnect with your body. Learning to embrace change now will help you in the future.

Of course, as your body's changing, so is your emotional world. You may worry that you're "behind" or "ahead" of where you're supposed to be in the process. But remember, everyone's timeline is their own, and you're exactly where God wants you to be.

Here's the most important part—even when things feel chaotic, your body was designed by God. He's the potter, and you're the clay. Every complex process of puberty is part of his intricate design, and because God is trustworthy, you can trust the process. When you pause to marvel at how God created you, you'll begin to see his intentionality in what looked like chaos.

Your body isn't a stranger. It's a masterpiece in progress, crafted by the Creator himself. Learning to love your body in all of its complexity isn't instant—it's a lifelong process. As you lean into God's truth, watch how he helps you see your body in a whole new way.

1. How have the physical changes of puberty felt for you so far? What are some emotions you've worked through?

2. When was the last time you felt amazed at how your body works? How does recognizing God's design in your body help you see it differently?

3. How do comments from others about your body affect you? How can you remind yourself of God's truth when that happens?

4. What steps can you take to see your body as a masterpiece in progress rather than something unfamiliar or flawed?

5. Knowing we're not alone on this journey can bring so much peace. Who do you feel comfortable talking to about the changes your body is experiencing?

PRAYER God, it can be hard to feel confident in my body when I don't even recognize it sometimes. Help me to remember that my body is the home you've given me on this earth, and give me grace to see all the changes in this season through your eyes. Thank you for being a kind, trustworthy Creator who is always in control.

So God created mankind in his own image, in the image of God he created them; male and female he created them.

GENESIS 1:27

WEEK 42

Even when the world treats girls unfairly, we are God's image-bearers.

I was watching a football game recently—a sport where most of the faces on the screen are men. But when the camera turned to a female staff member on the sidelines, someone immediately said, "What's going on with her eyebrows?" After watching male faces on the screen for hours with zero comments about their looks, one glance at a woman's face prompted immediate criticism.

As women and girls, it can feel like our bodies are constantly on display for evaluation and critique—from men and women alike. And this is just one way that sexism shows up in our everyday lives. Maybe you've noticed a lack of female representation in certain careers or stereotypical roles on TV, movies, and ads. On a personal level, maybe you've faced unfair dress code policies, unequal household responsibilities, sexual harassment, or objectification.

One of the most frustrating things about sexism is the shame it can bring—as if we somehow did something wrong to be treated unfairly. I experienced harassment several times as a young woman, but I didn't feel safe to stand up for myself. Those moments left an odd feeling in the pit of my stomach:

deep discomfort and shame, even though I did nothing wrong. Those experiences, over time, can even make us start to question our value.

Jesus' ministry on earth showed radical respect, care, and value for women. He spoke to, taught, and healed women in ways that broke the cultural norms of that time. He entrusted them with vital roles in his ministry, valuing them for their faith and humanity instead of reducing them to a one-dimensional role.

This week's verse is clear: God made both man and woman in his image, equally reflecting his glory and character. Women and girls aren't second-class citizens in God's kingdom, no matter how the world treats us. God calls each of us to reflect his image, walk by faith, and live out the purpose he's called us to—free from the shame and unjust treatment the world tries to impose.

1. When have you noticed or experienced sexism, and how did it make you feel?
2. Have you ever felt shame after being treated unfairly? If so, how can knowing the way God sees, loves, and values you as a woman help you overcome it?
3. How does knowing you're made in God's image change the way you see yourself?

PRAYER God, thank you for creating me with deep intentionality. I pray that you would help me to see the beauty in how you've created me and to remain secure in who I am in you, even when I'm treated unfairly. Remind me of my value when society makes me feel less than who I am and help me to stand up for girls and women everywhere so that we are all treated with dignity as your beloved daughters.

When I struggle with mood swings, I can rely on God's help.

I can't count the number of times I've felt irritated or depressed for days on end and then, like clockwork, my period starts. "Well, that explains a lot," I say to myself every time.

If you've started your period, you know the mood swings that come with it can feel overwhelming. In the days leading up to your cycle, you might feel irritable, angry, depressed, hopeless, or all of the above. These emotions, driven by the fluctuating hormones in your body, can feel out of control—making it hard to be kind and compassionate to others and to ourselves.

Thankfully, God hasn't left us powerless in the face of these challenges. The struggles we experience with premenstrual syndrome (PMS) are a reminder of a bigger truth about life: our emotions, whether they come from hormones or circumstances, don't have to rule us. When we feel like we "can't do it," God is reminding us to lean on his strength instead of our own. And when we take our emotions out on the people around us, he empowers us to humbly ask for forgiveness.

Be kind and compassionate to one another, forgiving each other, just as in Christ God forgave you.

EPHESIANS 4:32

112

Here are four tips for accessing God's grace during your monthly cycle:

* Just as God is kind and patient with you, extend that same grace to yourself. Be gentle with yourself, adjust your expectations, and be quick to ask for forgiveness (from both God and others) when you sin. Once you've done that, forgive yourself, too.
* Prepare yourself for the ups and downs. Tracking your cycle using a calendar or app can help you anticipate mood swings. Knowing what's ahead allows you to plan for extra rest and to think before you speak or act.
* Remember that you're in charge, not your emotions. Your feelings are very real and valid, but they're not always truthful guides. Take them as signals to reflect on and bring to God, rather than instructions to follow.
* Pause and choose your response. Intense emotions often feel urgent—like you need to act on them immediately. But with God's help, you can press pause, take a deep breath, and pray. Ask God to help you respond with love and patience—and to ask for forgiveness when you fall short.

PMS is tough, but it's also a reminder that we don't have to go through life—or our emotions—alone. Through his Spirit, God gives us the grace and strength to extend kindness to those around us and to ourselves, no matter how we feel.

1. How do you usually respond to intense emotions?
2. When was the last time you paused to pray before reacting to an overwhelming emotion? How did it change your response?

3. In what ways can you be kinder and more patient with yourself during challenging times?

4. Do you feel "out of control" when PMS comes? How could bringing your feelings to God help you rely on his strength more?

PRAYER God, I thank you that when I feel weak, you're giving me an opportunity to rely on your strength. Please help me to follow the Holy Spirit's leading instead of my emotions, even when it's difficult. Thank you that you are my Creator, so I can trust you to guide me through hormonal changes and anything else that comes my way.

God cares about my emotional well-being.

This passage feels like a warm hug from Jesus. On days when I feel anxious or weighed down, this promise of rest for my soul reminds me that Jesus is near, he cares deeply, and he offers comfort no matter how overwhelming life feels.

When we feel down or hopeless, our minds can trick us into thinking that no one truly understands. If it's hard for you to open up about how you're feeling, you might feel even more isolated, like no one really sees you. But God knows exactly what you're going through, and he will meet you right where you are.

I remember a time of deep grief when I sat in my car, playing a gospel song on repeat. I couldn't find the words to pray—only sobs. But as the music filled the space around me, I could feel God meeting me in the words of the song, the release of my tears, and the heavy feeling slowly lifting off my chest. In that moment, I knew I wasn't carrying my grief on my own.

When you face difficult emotions, remember that you're never alone. Even when you're totally convinced that you are, God is with you, and there are others out there who face similar struggles. Convincing ourselves that "no one understands" can

"Come to me, all you who are weary and burdened, and I will give you rest. Take my yoke upon you and learn from me, for I am gentle and humble in heart, and you will find rest for your souls. For my yoke is easy and my burden is light."

MATTHEW 11: 28–30

115

close us off from the support we desperately need. Tell a trusted adult how you're feeling—they may not have all the answers, but they can listen, pray with you, and help you find more support if you need it.

Support can look different for everyone. We can bring our burdens to God in prayer, lean on our faith community, or talk to a trusted loved one. Professional counselors, therapists, and doctors can also be part of the healing process. And for those of us with diagnosed depression or anxiety, medication can be a valuable tool. God can work through all of these approaches, and seeking help isn't a lack of faith—it's one of the ways God provides healing.

We all go through hard days and seasons, and struggling doesn't mean you're weak. Taking care of your mental health is part of caring for the whole person God created you to be. Learning about how your mind and body work (psychoeducation) can help you understand yourself and give yourself more grace on your journey.

Jesus cares about every part of you—your mind, heart, and soul. You don't have to carry your burdens alone. He invites you to find rest in him, to lay down the weight, and to let him hold what feels too heavy to bear.

1. When you read this week's verse, what emotions or thoughts come to mind?
2. What burdens are you carrying right now? Have you shared them honestly with God? If not, spend some time praying about how you've been feeling.
3. Who in your life is a trusted person you could reach out to when you're struggling? How can you take steps to open up to them?

4. Does the idea that God provides help in many forms—like counselors or medication—change the way you think about finding support when you're struggling?

5. What is one practical way you can care for yourself on hard days?

PRAYER God, I'm so grateful for your kind, gentle love. When I'm weary and don't know where to turn, please help me lean into your loving arms. And when I can't find the words to pray, remind me that you're always by my side, offering me the comfort, guidance, and hope that only you can provide.

Now listen, you who say, "Today or tomorrow we will go to this or that city, spend a year there, carry on business and make money." Why, you do not even know what will happen tomorrow. What is your life? You are a mist that appears for a little while and then vanishes. Instead, you ought to say, "If it is the Lord's will, we will live and do this or that."

JAMES 4:13–15

WEEK 45

Even when I'm feeling pressure to "succeed," I can trust God fully with my future.

Whenever she's making plans, my dear friend's grandmother always finishes her sentence the same way: ". . . if the Lord says the same." Her eyes twinkle with a wisdom that comes from a lifetime of walking with God through unexpected blessings and heart-shattering tragedies. Experience has humbled her, and she's fully embraced that her future is in God's hands, not her own.

Most of us who haven't lived quite as long can still tend to think we have much more control than we actually do. As a teen, teachers and guidance counselors made me feel like success would only come if I followed the perfect step-by-step plan. I felt like there was some recipe that had to be followed perfectly or else the whole future I'd envisioned would crumble. The pressure to get the best grades, excel in extracurriculars, and secure a spot at the "best" school can feel like either you win, or you're doomed. I wish someone had told me, "Either way, you'll be okay."

The truth is, life rarely unfolds the way we expect. There's no single path to success—and even "success" itself can look very different, depending on how you choose to define it. I know people whose paths unfolded exactly as they'd planned, only to regret their career choice later. I know others who switched majors, transferred schools, or took unexpected detours, only to discover a life they genuinely love. God's plans are much better than anything we could have scripted for ourselves, and he will help you grow into who you're meant to be—your Creator isn't restricted by where (or if) you go to college.

If you're feeling the pressure to succeed—whether from yourself or from others—remember this: God has already written every single page of your story. You can't mess up his plan because every detour you take is met with his grace and provision. When you surrender your plans to him, he will help you focus on cultivating a life of peace, joy, and faithfulness to him—a life you can be proud of, wherever it takes you.

1. What does "success" mean to you? Where do you think that definition comes from? How would God define success?
2. What pressures do you feel right now about the future? How can you bring them to God in prayer?
3. Have you ever experienced a moment when things didn't work out according to your plan, but God still worked it all out? How can that encourage you to trust him?

PRAYER God, I confess that sometimes the pressure to be successful makes me fear the future or feels like a heavy weight on my shoulders. I need your help to truly place my future in your hands and trust that you have a much bigger and more beautiful vision of my life than I ever could. Help me to focus on being faithful to you and a good steward of the gifts you've given me, trusting that you'll work out the rest.

Living with integrity brings glory to God.

> *Whoever walks in integrity walks securely, but whoever takes crooked paths will be found out.*
>
> **PROVERBS 10:9**

When I think of the people I admire most, there's one trait they all have in common: integrity. They may have very different passions and personalities, but what makes them stand out is how they stay true to their values. They're honest, keep their word, and make decisions based on God's truth, even when it's not the easiest or most popular choice. Their lives stand out because they're consistent and authentic—refreshing qualities in a world that often values appearances over character.

Integrity is about living according to the values God has instilled in us, no matter who's watching. But we aren't born knowing how to do this well! A friend I deeply admire shared that she once cheated on a big exam because she was eager to join the advanced math class that all her closest friends were in. She was already struggling in math, and she felt insecure and out of place among her friends. She thought cheating would solve that problem, but when she passed the exam and joined her friends' class, she struggled even more—eventually getting moved back down to the regular class anyway. Even though she never got "caught," she learned the hard way that compromising on God's values never leads to our ultimate good.

We sometimes think that as long as we can "get away with" a lie or other sin, we've avoided the consequences. But choosing to sin impacts us whether or not we're "caught". These choices weaken our convictions, harm our sense of self, and steal opportunities to glorify God with our actions.

God offers forgiveness for every mistake, and he also offers us help to live out his values. Small, everyday choices—like admitting when you're wrong, following through on your promises, or standing up for someone being mistreated—are acts of integrity. These may seem insignificant, but in a world full of sin, they shine like beacons of light.

Living with integrity isn't easy. It often requires standing out or choosing the harder path. But this week's verse reminds us that walking in integrity leads to security. There's a peace and confidence that comes from knowing your actions align with God's truth.

On the other hand, when we take "crooked paths"—compromising our values—those choices eventually catch up with us, and we're left needing to repair harm and rebuild trust with our loved ones.

Integrity isn't about being perfect; it's about pursuing God consistently, admitting when you fall short, and aligning your heart with his. When you choose to reflect God's character, even when no one is watching, you build trust with those around you and bring God glory.

1. Who in your life represents integrity to you? What qualities about them stand out?

2. Are there areas in your life where you feel tempted to compromise your God-given values? How can you ask God for help to stay true to him in those moments?

3. How do you handle moments when you make mistakes? How can admitting when you're wrong and seeking God's forgiveness help you grow?

4. Are you more tempted to compromise when you think no one will notice? How can you grow in evaluating your choices based on what God thinks, even when no one else is watching?

PRAYER God, I want to be a person of integrity—someone my loved ones can trust and, most of all, someone who honors you in my choices. When I'm tempted to compromise what I know is right, please help me to stand firm in what your Word says. Remind me that there is so much peace, joy, and security in living true to your values.

God empowers me to stand up for myself and his values.

Part of maturing in faith is finding your voice—building confidence in who you are in Christ and courageously standing for what aligns with his values.

I learned this firsthand as a high school freshman. I said yes to a relationship out of social pressure, not genuine feelings. Soon after, an over-the-top gesture on Valentine's Day made me feel uneasy and helped me realize I had agreed to a relationship that my heart wasn't ready for. I ended it soon after, and some people judged me harshly for doing so. But protecting my heart, knowing what I was and wasn't ready for, and honoring my intuition was the right choice for my well-being.

In this week's passage, five sisters approached Moses as he divided the Promised Land among Israel's tribes. They spoke up for themselves when their inheritance was at risk, and God affirmed their boldness, granting them the land they requested. Their story reminds us that advocating for ourselves, though uncomfortable at times, can be a means to experience God's care.

Self-advocacy might look like, "Please don't joke about that—it's a sensitive topic," or respectfully

"Why should our father's name disappear from his clan because he had no son? Give us property among our father's relatives." So Moses brought their case before the Lord, and the Lord said to him, "What Zelophehad's daughters are saying is right. You must certainly give them property as an inheritance among their father's relatives and give their father's inheritance to them."

NUMBERS 27:4–7

sharing your perspective with someone in authority. Advocating for yourself can feel vulnerable, since it affirms your worth and expresses your needs. But, like a muscle, your confidence will grow stronger with practice.

While following Jesus often requires prioritizing others, God also values our well-being and wants us to thrive. As you grow in discernment, he will help you navigate when to speak up and when to step back. Pay attention to the intuition God places in your heart—it's often his way of guiding you.

The next time you feel a strong gut feeling, bring your concerns to God in prayer. Trust him to guide you as you discern the next steps and find the courage to advocate for yourself. God will empower you to speak truth with confidence and grace.

1. Have you ever felt pressured to go along with something that didn't align with your values? How did you respond?
2. Think about a time when you ignored your God-given intuition. What was the outcome?
3. When you feel discomfort or unease in a situation, how can you discern whether it's God guiding you to advocate for yourself?
4. How can you balance the value of putting others first with allowing God to care for your well-being?

PRAYER God, I need your wisdom to learn how to use my voice in a healthy, confident way. When I'm afraid to speak up, remind me that the values you've given me, and my own well-being, are worth standing up for.

I need to take ownership of my walk with Jesus.

Some people think faith can be inherited—like sharing your parents' eye color or height. But faith doesn't "run in the family." Each one of us must decide for ourselves whether we will put our faith in Jesus.

If you have Christian parents, you may have relied on them a lot in your faith journey so far—and that's a blessing! But as you grow more independent in other areas of life, the same goes for your faith. This week's passage shows us that when faith is "alive," it's accompanied by action. Godly role models can set a strong foundation, but it's your responsibility to take the next steps and live out your faith. For me, this looked like finding a church that helped me connect with God, surrounding myself with friends who also loved Jesus, finding books about faith (along with the Bible, of course!) to help me learn more, and looking for opportunities to live out my faith by serving others, like this week's verse emphasizes.

The more I made my faith my own, the more exciting it became. I wasn't just following rules—I was building a real relationship with God that filled my life with peace and purpose. Whether or not

Suppose a brother or a sister is without clothes and daily food. If one of you says to them, "Go in peace; keep warm and well fed," but does nothing about their physical needs, what good is it? In the same way, faith by itself, if it is not accompanied by action, is dead.

JAMES 2:15–17

your parents are believers, the keys to keeping your faith alive are the same:

* Stay curious. It's tempting to skim over familiar Bible passages, thinking you've heard it all before. But God's Word is living and active, and he always has something new to show you. Ask questions, dig deeper, and look for new ways to apply Scripture to your life.

* Be honest about your doubts. Faith doesn't mean you understand everything and agree without a second thought. I've been a Christian for almost 20 years now, and I still have SO many questions! But every time I bring my doubts to God, I end up feeling closer to him—even if I still don't quite understand it all. God is never offended by our questions; he welcomes them because they show that we want to get to know him better.

* When in doubt, pray. Sometimes, we feel like we've drifted away from God. We stop opening our Bibles, attending church, or talking about him with others. When that happens, don't wait until you feel "ready" to come back. Just pray. You don't need the perfect words—just have an honest conversation with God, telling him how you're feeling and asking him to draw you closer to him.

Faith is built by small actions each day, like a house being built brick by brick. As you take ownership of your walk with Jesus, you'll see your faith grow stronger and more joyful than ever before.

1. If you come from a Christian family, have you ever felt like you're relying on their faith instead of growing in your own walk with Jesus?
2. What is some evidence that your faith is alive and active?

3. What's one question or doubt you've been afraid to bring to God? How can you start that conversation with him today?
4. Who in your life sets an example of faith that's "alive"? How can you learn from their actions?

PRAYER God, you see me and know me. If there's any part of my faith that's been on autopilot, I pray that you would wake me up and empower me to build a faith that's alive and active. When I start skimming instead of really soaking in your Word, stop me and help me to see with fresh eyes. And when I have doubts, let my questions draw me closer to you. Thank you for always being ready to receive me with open arms.

When life doesn't make sense, I can still trust God.

> "For my thoughts are not your thoughts, neither are your ways my ways," declares the LORD. "As the heavens are higher than the earth, so are my ways higher than your ways and my thoughts than your thoughts."
>
> **ISAIAH 55:8–9**

Tragedy. Suffering. Loss. Injustice. So often, life leaves us crying out, "God, I don't understand. This makes no sense."

When life feels unfair and senseless, a part of me wants to give up hope. The only thing that keeps me holding on is the truth in this week's verse: that even when we're confused, God isn't. When we can't see how God could possibly redeem our painful circumstances, he is already working in the midst of them. And even when circumstances don't change, God is present—not distant and uncaring, but right beside us, feeling our every heartache and surrounding us with his comfort.

When I struggle to believe this, I think back to my friend Phillip. He passed away suddenly at just 19 years old, but a few hours before his death, he led his church in prayer. His words still echo in my heart:

"You are amazing, Lord, and so often we spend too much time trying to figure you out. The good things we stare at, and we forget to thank you. We look at bad things that happen and ask, 'Why did this happen, Lord?' We forget that you have a plan. We know that in darkness and light, in good times and bad times, you are there! We can just sit back and not worry! We may not know what tomorrow may bring, but we know it is your will and as long as we know that, it is okay. Even in the midst of a storm on a sinking ship, it is good, and I know it is good."

Phillip prayed these words from a heart that knew suffering—he lost his mother to violence at a young age—yet he trusted that God's light could pierce even the darkest moments. So even though his death felt completely senseless, painful, and unfair, I couldn't deny the power of his last words to us. Phillip's prayer convinced me that God is *always* present, good, and loving—even in the deepest tragedies—and his words became a turning point for my faith, wrapping me in comfort, even as we grieved his death.

I don't know the tragedies you've experienced or witnessed that break your heart and test your faith. But I do know this—God's heart breaks with yours, and from the depth of his care for you, he is unfolding his plan, even when you can't understand it yet. God already knows the end of the story and sees far beyond what we can. One day, we'll see God face-to-face, and our confusion will melt away. In the meantime, you can trust him to hold you, comfort you, and bring beauty out of even the hardest circumstances.

1. When have you faced a situation that made no sense to you? How did it affect your faith in God?
2. Do you find it difficult to trust God when circumstances don't change? How can this week's verse encourage you?
3. Think of a time when you saw beauty come from a painful situation. How did that experience impact your faith?

4. How can you remind yourself of God's faithfulness when life feels confusing, overwhelming, or unfair?

PRAYER God, I pray for a faith that trusts in your goodness, even in the midst of a storm. When I'm confused and heartbroken, help me to feel you holding me and wiping my tears, and remind me that you exist far above even the most difficult situations. Even when my questions remain unanswered, help my heart rest in the knowledge that you care, and that you are always working for my good and your glory.

The blessings of living for God are far greater than any earthly blessing.

I love the Psalms because they're refreshingly honest, and they tackle questions that we still wrestle with today. I often struggle with the reality that doing things "right" doesn't mean I'll get every earthly thing I desire. I get frustrated when I can't afford something I really want, while others have more money than they know what to do with. It feels so unfair!

In this week's passage, God, through the psalmist, addresses this question by reminding us of the bigger picture. When we zoom out from what we currently see, we realize that earthly prosperity doesn't last. The wealth, popularity, and pleasures of this world are fleeting, like grass that grows for a while but then withers away.

Unfortunately, many of us are taught (either directly or indirectly) that following Jesus leads to a life of earthly blessings: health, wealth, success, and comfort. Because God is good, our human logic assumes that we'll only experience things that we consider good. But the truth is, in our world full of sin, none of us can avoid pain or challenges. Jesus

Do not fret because of those who are evil or be envious of those who do wrong; for like the grass they will soon wither, like green plants they will soon die away. Trust in the LORD and do good; dwell in the land and enjoy safe pasture. Take delight in the LORD, and he will give you the desires of your heart.

PSALM 37:1–4

never promised an easy or prosperous life. He promised something better—himself.

You may feel frustrated as you make hard decisions to live for Jesus—saying no to things that are tempting or popular, standing firm in your faith when it's easier to go with the flow, or choosing integrity when dishonesty would bring quicker results. You may wonder what the point is of living for God if others seem to be doing fine without him. But looks can be deceiving.

The happiness that comes from living for yourself is short-lived. The parties end, the applause fades, and the short-term pleasure of sin ends up leaving us empty. But the joy that comes from our relationship with Jesus lasts. When I'm focused on growing closer to God, I find myself less caught up in how "unfair" life seems, and more grounded in gratitude for the unshakable joy I have in him. It's a joy that doesn't depend on my circumstances, and has anchored me through every high and low.

When you "delight in the Lord" as this week's passage invites us, you'll find that he transforms the desires of your heart. The things that once seemed important, like material comforts and blessings, lose their grip as you realize the greater blessings that come from walking with God: peace, purpose, hope, and his unconditional love.

1. Have you ever felt envious of someone else whose life seemed more "blessed," even though they weren't following Jesus? How did it affect your relationship with God?
2. Have you ever experienced God transforming the desires of your heart? What did that look like?
3. Do you think you've been placing too much value on earthly blessings or rewards? How can you shift your focus?

4. When you lose motivation to live for Jesus, how can his promise of lasting joy encourage you?

PRAYER God, I want to experience the joy of living for you. Help me to run my own race instead of looking left and right at what other people are doing. Please help me to be content with a life that honors you and to embrace the blessings of your peace, hope, joy, and love that are always available to me by your grace.

God's truth is a firm foundation, even when it seems like "truth" is up for debate.

But in your hearts revere Christ as Lord. Always be prepared to give an answer to everyone who asks you to give the reason for the hope that you have. But do this with gentleness and respect, keeping a clear conscience, so that those who speak maliciously against your good behavior in Christ may be ashamed of their slander.

1 PETER 3:15–16

The world is full of opinions, and society often claims that we can decide our own truth and moral compass. While this idea may sound freeing, deep down, we know there must be a foundational truth that doesn't shift with trends or arguments. So how do you "give the reason for the hope that you have" when truth seems to be up for debate?

At some point, you'll encounter people or ideas that challenge your faith. Through conversations, social media, or music and movies, society often tells us that morality is subjective: that everyone can decide what's right and wrong for themselves.

But as Christians, we know that the Bible isn't just another opinion. It's God's Word (2 Timothy 3:16–17), a guide that reveals who God is and how he calls us to live. The Bible's firm foundation provides stability in an ever-changing world.

When someone questions your beliefs, you don't need to have all the answers. I love a good debate, and sometimes a healthy one can help both people grow. But what I love most about our Christian faith is that it promises a personal, intimate relationship with God through Jesus. So even when I'm stumped by a question about my faith, I can share confidently about my personal experience—the peace Jesus gives me, the way he's transformed me, and the hope he provides. No argument can take away the reality of your experience with God, and any questions you face can inspire you to dive deeper in the Bible for insight.

Remember, actions speak louder than words. Some people in our lives may see Christianity as outdated, or they may have had a bad experience with Christians in the past. For these people, your kindness and authenticity can offer a fresh perspective, giving them their first glimpse of God's love. Our gentleness and respect can speak volumes as we trust God to move in the lives of the people around us.

1. What does it mean to you that the Bible is a firm foundation?
2. How does your personal experience with Jesus give you confidence in your faith?
3. Who in your life might benefit from seeing an authentic example of Christ's love?
4. How can you live boldly for Christ and gently address questions without feeling the pressure to "win" arguments?

PRAYER God, I'm so grateful that your Word provides a sure foundation for me to stand on. When the world challenges my faith, I pray that you would help me stand secure in the relationship I have with you through Jesus. Help me to represent you with gentleness and respect, reflecting your character to those around me. I trust that you can use me to shine the light of your truth and love in my community.

Every good and perfect gift is from above, coming down from the Father of the heavenly lights, who does not change like shifting shadows.

JAMES 1:17

In a season when everything seems to be changing, we can trust our unchanging God.

Adolescence is a whirlwind season of change. Even in the months since you began this devotional, you've probably experienced unexpected twists and turns. Friendships may have shifted, some growing deeper while others faded. Your relationships with your parents or siblings might feel more complicated. Your body is changing, and hormones can take you on an emotional roller coaster. You're wrestling with big questions about who you are, what you believe, and where your life is headed. It can feel like everything is in flux.

But in the midst of all this uncertainty, we have this comforting truth: God never changes.

Unlike shadows that move with every shift of the sun, God remains steady and constant. You never have to wonder if God will show up when you need him—he will. You don't have to question if he'll forgive you when you fall short—he promises to, every time. You don't have to worry whether he has good plans for your future—he's already written them with care and purpose. Even as seasons come and go, God is unchanging, always present, and completely faithful. His promises will always remain true, no matter what these months and years to come may bring.

The morning after my high school graduation, I sobbed. I was excited to move across the country for college, but I wasn't ready to leave my friends, family, and community behind. On move-in day, I felt completely alone and deeply out of place: a Midwest girl from a working-class family suddenly dropped into a room full of East Coast kids from elite prep schools.

But from day one, God brought the right friends into my new life—some who felt out of place too, and others who surprised me with how much we had in common. I found joyful, faith-filled, lifelong friends who still love me and pray for me to this day. When I look back at how God provided for me, I'm reminded of how faithful he is during every transition.

No matter how your life changes, you will always remain God's child because of your faith in Jesus. He will always listen when you pray, meet you with kindness and compassion, and provide for your needs. And even when his answers to your prayers aren't what you expected, he will always be walking beside you, working for your ultimate good.

In a world where so much feels uncertain, let God be your anchor. The same God who made the stars and holds them in place also holds you—and that will never change.

1. What changes in your life feel the most destabilizing right now?
2. How does the promise that God is unchanging bring you comfort?
3. How can you remind yourself of God's unchanging love when it feels like everything else is shifting?

4. How can you share the hope of an unchanging God with a friend who might also feel overwhelmed right now?

PRAYER God, sometimes the changes all around me feel overwhelming, and I'm not sure what I can hold on to. Please show me what a steady foundation you are, and help me to cling to you for stability. Thank you that no matter what is happening, you are trustworthy, dependable, and able to meet my every need.

Resources

Here are a few resources I recommend to strengthen your walk with God:

The Jesus I Wish I Knew in High School, edited by Cameron Cole and Charlotte Getz

My Utmost for His Highest by Oswald Chambers

New Morning Mercies for Teens by Paul David Tripp

Acknowledgments

I am constantly in awe of the way God shows up to help me when I need it most. I asked him for wisdom, strength, and energy to write these pages, and he met me with his grace every step of the way. Thank you, Lord!

To my husband: there are no words that could capture your sacrificial love, not only during this writing process but always. Thank you for pouring your whole heart into supporting me, and for all your wisdom and encouragement that made this book possible.

To Keziah, Koimburi, and Ezekiel: you three bring me more joy than I ever could have imagined. Thank you for being patient with me as I wrote, and a special thank-you to Keziah for being so eager to help. I had future-you in mind as I wrote every word.

To my parents and siblings: thank you for encouraging me to develop my gifts and pursue my dreams at every age. A special thank-you to my mom—you Grandma'd your heart out so I could have more time to write, and I'm forever grateful!

To Fatimah, one of the wisest humans I know: this book would not be what it is without your gospel-centered, heartfelt contributions. Thank you for carving out the time—your insights had an incredible impact on these pages.

To Marissa and Carolyn: what would I do without my "DNA"? Thank you for being a source of stability, wisdom, support, and discipleship, and for the priceless perspective that each of you brought to portions of this book.

To Pastor Tommy and Pastor Terrance: thank you for your many years of faithful service and for shepherding my family with such genuine love. I drew so much spiritual strength for this writing process from your preaching and pastoral care.

To each of my precious friends: your love sustains me. Thank you for always lifting me up.

To everyone at Zeitgeist: thank you for this incredible opportunity and for your guidance throughout the process. Jennifer and Kim, your insightful edits and suggestions strengthened every page of this book.

To Chelsea Goodan and Donna Jackson Nakazawa: your books on teen girlhood gave me a vital perspective on the unique challenges that teen girls face today. Thank you for your empowering, strengths-based findings that informed my approach to this book.

To the teens (and former teens) who so graciously shared their honest thoughts with me on these topics: thank you for your generosity and vulnerability. I admire you more than you know!

And finally, to every teen reading this book: you inspire me, truly. As I researched and prayed my way through this writing process, I found myself in awe of everything you have to carry. Life isn't easy, and your desire to follow Jesus as you navigate the ups and downs of these years is beautiful to witness. Thank you for allowing me to walk a bit of this journey with you.

01 14
√

About the Author

Ellie Hunja is an author, social worker, wife, and mother of three living in Los Angeles. Her writing flows from her deep love of people and aims to cultivate connection, build empathy, and inspire growth.

She grew up in Southfield, Michigan, and attended Georgetown University, where she earned a BA in sociology, and the University of Michigan, where she earned a master's of social work. She has always been passionate about the mental and spiritual health of kids and teens, and she currently serves with the youth ministry at her church, One Church Lakewood.

She is the author of *Blessings, New Mom: A Women's Devotional*, which offers biblical encouragement for moms during their baby's first year. She has also contributed to websites such as Her View from Home, Thought Catalog, Equipping Godly Women, and The Mighty, as well as in print for *TheMomCo* magazine and the book *So God Made a Mother*.

Ellie loves museums, musical theater, Motown music, and making memories with her family. You can find more of her writings at EllieHunja.com, where she covers topics like parenting, faith, mental health, social justice, raising autistic children, and more.

Connect with Ellie on Instagram @elliehunja and Facebook @elliehunjawriter.

Hi there,

We hope you enjoyed *Teen Devotional for Girls*. If you have any questions or concerns about your book, or have received a damaged copy, please contact customerservice@penguinrandomhouse.com. We're here and happy to help.

Also, please consider writing a review on your favorite retailer's website to let others know what you thought of the book!

Sincerely,
The Zeitgeist Team